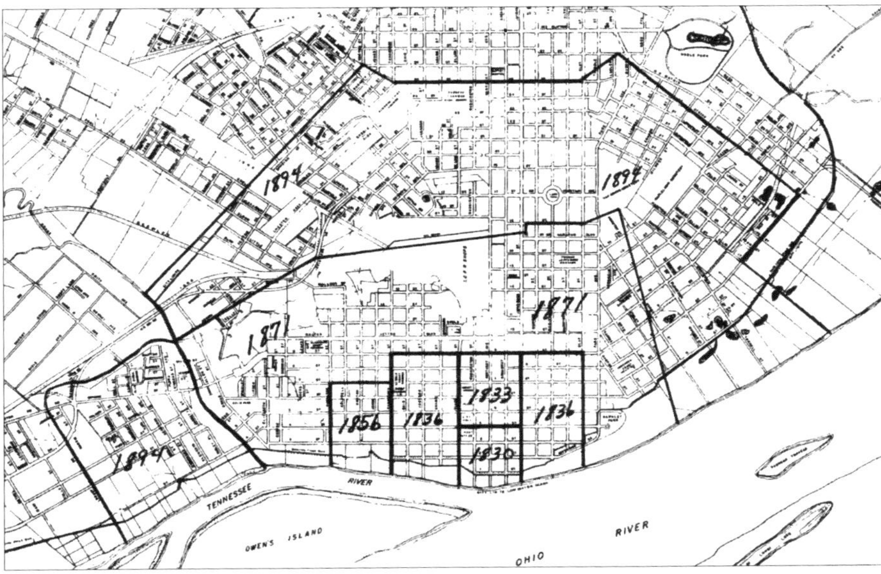

Paducah city map.

PADUCAH KENTUCKY

A HISTORY

JOHN E.L. ROBERTSON
WITH ANN E. ROBERTSON

THE History PRESS

Published by The History Press
Charleston, SC 29403
www.historypress.net

Front cover, lower image: Robert Dafford floodwall mural,
used with the consent of Dafford Murals.

Back cover, bottom left: NC-4, November 17, 1919.
Image courtesy of Engineer Office, City of Paducah.
Bottom right: From "Flowers of the Crown" by artist Shirley P. Kelly.
Courtesy of the National Quilt Museum

First published 2014

Manufactured in the United States

ISBN 978.1.62619.532.5

Library of Congress CIP data applied for.

CONTENTS

PREFACE

There are two Paducahs: one in Kentucky and one in Texas. In Kentucky, an elaborate myth has grown over time concerning the origin of the name. According to one of the more common variants, Chief Paduke was a Chickasaw who owned the land at the mouth of the Tennessee River and returned to the site after it had been ceded to the whites under the Clark claim. According to this version, the old Indian died and was buried here by his grieving followers. So noble and distinguished was this savage that William Clark decided to rename the village of Pekin in honor of the chief.

A statue of the legendary Chief Paduke was commissioned by the Daughters of the American Revolution in 1909. Lorenzo Taft was the artist who made the carving, and he got to thinking about the Indian and wanted to know more about him; therefore, Taft wrote to some of the leading authorities of the time, inquiring about Paduke. Taft became convinced that the whole story was a fabrication and reported as much to Chicago newspapers. Word of Taft's revelation reached Paducah, and a wave of misguided public sentiment caused many to rise in defense of the city's symbol, including Irvin S. Cobb.

By the time of homecoming in 1913, Chief Paduke was officially declared to be a person by Paducahans. In fact, James Wheeler portrayed the legendary chief in the celebration; he arrived by river, rode up Broadway and received the official welcome of Mayor Thomas Needham Hazelip. In connection with the controversy, it is interesting to note that the Paducah newspapers carried

Left: William Clark bust.

Below: Robert Dafford mural showing (left to right) William Clark and George Rogers Clark's arrival at the site of Paducah.

Statue of legendary Chief Paduke by Loredo Taff.

a picture of Chief Paduke—a feat quite remarkable since Paduke was reported to have died in 1818, before photography was conceived. Bumptious behavior of Paducahans continued to add to the legend. From where, then, did the name of the city derive?

There are two other equally well-known legends of Paducah. Edmund Flagg, in *The Far West*, records the story of a captive Indian woman who was sacrificed by a band of Pawnees after having been assured of her safety.[1] At least the Skidi Pawnee have a legend of having lived in the Ohio Valley at one time; perhaps the two traditions became intermingled. The other story seems to have been the origin of the name given to the Kentucky community.

In *Letters of the Lewis and Clark Expedition with Related Documents, 1783–1854*, edited by Donald Jackson, there are numerous references to the "Padouca" tribe of Indians. James McKay considered the name Paduca synonymous with Madoc, a Welsh prince, and William Clark knew of McKay's map;[2] therefore, one of Clark's aims was to find some evidence of these "white" Indians. He did not find the main branch, but Clark wrote to Albert Gallatin on March 31, 1826, that "most of those bands alluded to in the relation to my voyage or the map annexed are the remnants of the once powerful nation of the Padoucas, now become so reduced that only a few bands are at this time known."[3]

In 1827, Clark wrote to his son M.L. Clark, a cadet at West Point, that he was on his way to the mouth of the Tennessee River to lay out a town named Paducah to honor the memory of a proud people who had been decimated by contact with European civilization.

Chapter 1

PADUCAH

In 1884, Robert S. Davis, who came to Paducah from Harrison County, Kentucky, in 1821, was interviewed. Davis recounted that the first house at the Paducah location was claimed by more than one party, and the title of William Clark was also questioned in the courts.

George Rogers Clark claimed the site of Paducah under a Virginia Treasury warrant dated September 15, 1795. Clark died in 1818, and it remained for his brother William, of Lewis and Clark fame, to develop the site. William Clark had the location platted on June 18, 1830.[4] In between, the state Supreme Court affirmed the Clark title.[5]

In 1827, the court at Louisville appointed Samuel Dickinson commissioner to carry out the sale of the Clark lands in western Kentucky. The record shows that William Clark purchased the site of Paducah. This was later found to have given a defective title, so the court corrected the record to show that the land was purchased by George Woolfolk of Shelbyville, Kentucky. The heirs of George Rogers Clark were instructed to deed the land to Woolfolk, and if they failed to do so, Samuel Dickinson, as commissioner, was ordered to "do it for them." The heirs did nothing; Dickinson acted on June 16, 1827. Woolfolk later sold the land to William Clark on October 13, 1827, for "the sum of five dollars in hand paid." Woolfolk seems to have acted in this matter as the agent of William Clark, a role that he would later play at Paducah. Finally, Clark's title was clean. Settlement could start.

The first election for trustees for Paducah was held on May 2, 1831, at the home of George Dunn. At the meeting of this first board three days later, F.A.

Lewis and Clark memorial by George Lundeen on the grounds of MAQS.

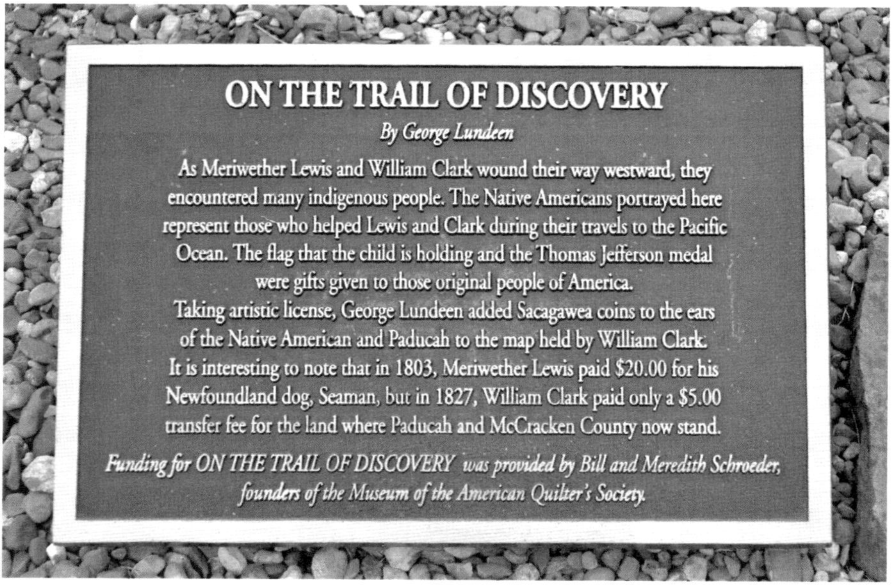

Plaque for Lundeen's Lewis and Clark statues.

Harrison was made chairman. Thomas J. Flournoy, George Dunn, Robert Enders and Dr. Robert Fletcher, the trustees, made Ruben Laughlin clerk and assessor, while James C. Calhoun became collector and Valentine Owen was selected the first overseer of streets. The first business included orders to remove fences standing across some public avenues and to prevent keelboats from landing in front of the town. The question of the city waterfront was to occupy the city leaders on many future occasions, as the presence of keelboats, broad horns, flat boats, rafts and, later, steamboats was to be both a source of revenue and a menace to the health of the community.[6]

All towns perform a service. Paducah developed as the center of commerce for the region. The vitality of the community, its organization and its growth depended on the town's role as the center of distribution of goods and services to the surrounding hinterland. Located as Paducah was on two major waterways, river trade was of prime importance to the growth of the town. In a short time, Paducah was a break-in-bulk point for much of the traffic on the lower Ohio River.

After the election held on June 15, 1833, James McPherson was the unanimous choice for chairman of the trustees, who now included John Hynes, David Smith, Archibald W. Taylor and John F. Harris. Braxton Small was the clerk (a post he also held in the county government), and Robert Enders became the town treasurer. Gustavus A. Flournoy was appointed assessor and was instructed to compile a list of all white males over twenty-one and all black males over sixteen for the purpose of a poll tax. In addition to this routine business, the board appointed a board of health.[7] The purpose of this panel was to ensure that sanitary conditions were observed in the town. The new board was to pay particular attention to conditions along the waterfront. If it discovered evidence indicating a hazard to the public, it was to require the supervisor of streets to take corrective measures. Itinerant craft that persisted in ignoring the basic sanitary measures were a thorn in the board's side and led to the banning of such craft from the area fronting on Water Street. Another reason for such a pronouncement was that the town profited from the sale of space along the riverfront to venders of wood for fuel on steamboats.

Nonresidents were denied the privilege of piling wood for sale on the public landing unless they paid the town collector a tax of 12.5 cents per cord.[8] Trade boats were not allowed to remain docked longer than twenty-four hours or they would face a fine of $2.50 and costs. All other craft were instructed to remove to the bayou just below the town or pay a fine of $2.00 and costs.[9]

Operation of the town wharf boat produced revenue for the town. The franchise was sold to Joseph H. Fowler.[10]

Local inhabitants evidently were equally lax in the disposal of their wastes. The board took cognizance of this fact by empowering the supervisor of Paducah to "proceed immediately under the superintendence of the Board of Health to remove, or destroy beyond the corporation or destroy all nuisancez [*sic*] which may be found in the streets."[11]

In addition to the primary roles of cities (defense, governmental administration, commerce, entertainment, etc.), they also provide residents with basic services. Among the elements in this infrastructure are waste disposal, water sources, fire protection, police protection, streets and supervision of local resources. For a long time, a reliable source of water was a pressing problem in Paducah and remained a perennial problem until 1884, when the city granted a private corporation the right to construct a modern system.[12] Piped water was an unknown luxury in 1833, when the trustees first had to deal with the problem of an adequate supply of drinking water. John Hynes and David Smith were authorized to let a contract for a public well. The minutes of the meeting also called for a "pump" with the well, but this evidently did not materialize, and a bucket had to serve for many years. The well required constant care. Frequently, the well had to be cleaned. For some reason, the life of buckets was notoriously short and caused the board much grief.[13]

Another community hazard was fire. The town was almost ruined by fire on several occasions—by accident in 1838 and 1852 and by design during the raid of Nathan Bedford Forrest during the War of the Rebellion. Concern with this ever-present threat to public safety dates from early 1833, when a special committee was appointed to inspect the chimney of a small house to ascertain whether any danger to neighboring structures existed. If it did, the commissioners were to have the chimney made safe. Conditions required a similar committee to reassess the conditions in 1834. Later, the committee reported back to the trustees that extensive renovation would be necessary among the waterfront lots, particularly those numbered one to twelve.[14] Later, the chairman of the board, William W. Lay, was authorized to let contracts for five hooks and two ladders.

Vigilance alone was not enough to safeguard property from fires. Immediately after the fire of 1838, G. Flournoy, John Wilson and S.B. Halsed were empowered to purchase a fire engine for the town.[15] Firefighting was to remain volunteer duty until 1882, and while willing, these amateurs could not cope with a major conflagration. The city did build a two-story brick fire station on what are now Third and Tennessee Streets in 1854 as a direct consequence of the disastrous blaze of 1852 that burned whole blocks.[16]

Being on a major transportation route, Paducah came into early contact with the world of entertainment. At a meeting of the board held on June 3, 1834, it was resolved that "no transit theatrical companies, vantriloquists [*sic*], or slight [*sic*] of hand performers, or men exhibiting wax figures, or caravans of animals, or any other exhibition or show be permitted to exhibit or perform without paying $5.00 in advance to the Supervisor."[17] Apparently, this fee did not deter shows, nor was it intended to prevent performers from entertaining in Paducah. R. Letton paid $12.50 to perform in Paducah in 1837. Other examples of the bill of fare available to audiences in the 1830s in Paducah include F.C. Combs, who was exhibiting human skulls and "a specimen of the fine arts" as an interesting combination of the lurid and the edifying. An anaconda was to be seen at the Rising Sun Tavern at the same time.[18]

Originally conceived in early 1836, the Paducah market was constructed by August of that year. It was then a frame structure that measured sixty feet in length by thirty-three feet in width. The cost was $464.50, not counting the replacement of the original wooden "pillows" with brick or the flooring, which came later. The market had a shingle roof and was weather boarded

Early market days in Paducah. *Courtesy of the William Clark Museum.*

and painted. C.C. Russell, E.J. Holliday and W.W. Lay were the accepting agency for the town.[19] Immediately, the market was put to use. Stalls in the market were rented on an annual basis, such as the right to use the northeast corner, which went to B.B. Jones for $8.00 per year.[20]

A monopoly was granted to the market to ensure that it would be successful. Fore selling was punishable by a fine of twenty dollars (trial by jury was permitted in all such cases arising from the ordinance). Market hours were from 4:00 a.m. until 7:00 p.m.[21] The post of market master originally went to Walter Padgett, who was quickly replaced by George Harrison.[22] A monopoly of auctioneering in the town was granted to Noah Fuqua in 1838.[23]

Paducah continued making internal improvements. Attention was given to the grading of streets,[24] construction and sidewalks,[25] paving of some streets in the business district[26] and improvement of the town's docking facilities.[27] These improvements were essential to the continued growth of Paducah from a rural community into a city.[28]

To meet the needs of its merchants, the town of Paducah set up a municipal bank to issue the necessary bills of exchange.[29] This agency of the town began operations in 1837 and issued bills ranging in value from 75 cents to 6¼ cents to a total of $500. These bills were redeemable at a ratio of one to five in the following currency: $100 in Kentucky bills, $200 in Alabama currency and $200 in bills from Tennessee. The treasurer of this institution was Braxton Small, who served as county clerk, as well as trustee of Paducah at various times.[30] This pioneer bank was called the Exchange Bank of Paducah.

Paducah reached its first plateau of growth with the change from village to third-class status achieved on March 10, 1856:

> *On the 25th of the ensuing August, an election was held to adopt the new charter making it a city, with the following result. For, 209 votes; against, thirty five. At the first election under the new charter, J.H. Gardner was chosen its mayor, and the several gentlemen mentioned hereafter were selected as councilmen: First Ward—A.G. Lee and D.A. Given; Second Ward—J.C. Walden and George A. Allen; Third Ward—William Enders and Gabriel Kay; Fourth Ward—O.G. Bullitt and Daniel Fourshee; Fifth Ward—T.J. Atkins and J.K. Leman; Sixth Ward—George Langstaff and W.H. Slack; George Smedley, police judge; W.L. McGary, assistant judge; John W. Sauner, marshall; W.L. Fuqua, deputy marshall; Q.Q. Quigley, attorney; Charles H. Bonnin, clerk; William F. Swift, assessor; M.W. Cole, treasurer; D.A. Maxwell, physician.*[31]

The remainder of the city posts were filled at the first meeting of the city council, held on May 11, 1857. Henry S. Lewis was appointed railroad tax collector; J.W. Sauner, city tax collector; George Dunn, market master; Henry Adams, wharf master; and J.S. Long, sexton. The appearance of the public official devoted to railroads is significant. That mode of transport was just beginning to supplant the steamboat as the principal carrier. The appearance of all-weather transportation coincided with the transformation of the community from a town into a city and continued to sustain the growth of Paducah into the late 1800s, when the city grew into a major railroad hub.[32]

Paducah progressed rapidly from 1830 until it became a third-class city in 1856. This was a period of growth, both in physical extent and in population. The raw census data for 1850 gives an interesting picture of Paducah. This data is the result of the census taken by N.M. McCurty and shows that the city of Paducah had 322 dwellings at this time. The total population included 374 slaves and 18 free Negroes. There were 1,141 males and 972 females. A cursory examination of the first 137 houses recorded by McCurty reveals that the social and economic patterns in Paducah tended to resemble those usually found in pre-industrial societies in that living arrangements seemed to be ordered on a master-apprentice relationship. For example, in the household of William Nolen, who was listed as a tinner and coppersmith, there resided two single men, Henry Timberlake and Berryman Heyman, ages twenty-two and twenty-three, respectively. Both gave their occupations to be that of tinner. With D.A. Given, a merchant, lived Augustus Hoeffner, J.G. Fowler and Samuel Wilson, all listed as clerks or storekeepers. B.J. Mills and T.H. Hill boarded with William W. Hart and, like him, listed their vocations as carpenter. John Grief was a blacksmith, as was his boarder, Joseph Sizemore. W.H. Puryear gave his trade as that of saddler, as did H.P. Robinson, twenty-seven, single and a resident in the house of Puryear. Evidence to prove that these boarders actually worked for their landlords is lacking, but it makes for strong assumption.[33]

Another fact is quickly revealed: there was a severe housing shortage in Paducah. Even those who list considerable property, both real and personal, often had several persons outside their immediate families living with them. In some instances, these are linked by nationality, as was the case of Leonard Roche. Not only were his next-door neighbors, Theophilous Roche and his wife and child, from France, but also in Leonard's house were to be found Leonard's wife and child, L. Girat (seventy-one, female), A. Chiron (twenty-six, male, farmer), Harris Gouart (thirty, male), one named Carpenter (thirty-three, male, laborer), one named Menil (nineteen, male laborer), Arma Charon (eighteen, female) and Augustine Gouart (seventy-two, male, farmer). The Irish congregated around P.S. Keith, a road surfacer, and his wife and daughter. With them resided eleven young, male laborers and one young female. It is not possible to establish the number of rooms in these houses, but it would seem that privacy was a rare thing in Paducah in 1850.[34]

Newspapers began in Paducah with the *Express*, published by R.R. Wills in about 1834–35. The political orientation was Whig, which reflected the difference between Paducah and the rest of the Purchase region. The Purchase developed the reputation for being the state's strongest bastion of Jacksonian Democracy; however, Paducah took an independent course until after the Civil War.

McKay Lambdin tried to establish another Whig journal in 1844. This paper was the *West Kentuckian*. The venture did not go well, and Lambdin sold out to William Grief, who had learned his trade on the *Express*. L.M. Flournoy and John W. Crockett served as editors (the latter being a nephew of Davie Crockett). Crockett was succeeded by J.R. Alexander. In 1849, this paper was sold to H.M. McCarty and R.W. Perry, who changed the name to the *Paducah Journal*. In 1855, they sold out to J. Stoddard Byers and Reverend W.W. Dodd, who leased the paper to D.W. McCarty and F.W. Thomas. Finally, in 1856, the paper failed.[35]

In 1851, the *Paducah Democrat* made its appearance under the leadership of C.C. Riley. The cost was two dollars per year. Later, R.B.J. Twyman became editor and enlarged the subscription list. Still, the paper was not without challengers. The *Pennant*, a Whig supporter, appeared in 1853. The *Pennant* was published by Samuel Pike until 1854, when it came into the hands of George H. Morrow, who kept it only a short time and transferred the title to Perry & McGoodwin. The latter firm changed the name to the *Paducah American* and supported the Know-Nothing Party. John D. McGoodwin also tried the *Paducah Sentinel*, a Whig paper, during this period. It came to nothing. A church organ, the *Christian Banner*, reported the views of elder J.R. Howard of the Christian Church for ten months. In 1857, John C. Noble started the *Paducah Herald*, a Democratic publication, which lasted until occupying forces of the Union closed it. Two other papers made brief appearances prior to the Civil War. These brave efforts were the *Commercial* in 1859, a Whig voice in what had become principally a Democratic wilderness, and the *Dollar Times*, published by W.L. Geary about 1857. The *Commercial* was edited and published by William Rollston.[36]

Paducah was not without culture in 1854. Family concerts were not uncommon, nor were performances by the local brass band. The *Paducah Daily Democrat* advertised that education was available for those who sought it. The school for young ladies conducted by Professor W.W. Dodge taught mental and moral sciences, mathematics, astronomy, geography, chemistry, natural philosophy, mineralogy, French and music and offered clothes washing to the students for a nominal fee.[37] The female seminary had been established on land donated by William Clark. Funding came, in part, from an act passed by the legislature in 1836 allowing lotteries to raise funds of $100,000 for general purposes. The money was to be distributed as follows: "One-half for establishing a male seminary, one-fourth for a female seminary, and one-fourth for a public wharf."[38] About $60,000 was raised in Paducah.

Subtle changes began to take place in Paducah during the 1840s and early 1850s. Merchandising and shipping still were growing in importance; however, two new forces made their appearance: the marine ways and the railroad. Elijah Murray of St. Louis contracted with the Town of Paducah to build a marine railway. The consideration was $1,000 for the patent and $500 for superintending the construction of the town's first permanent industry—one that has been in continuous operation ever since 1854, when the firm actually began operation. Ten years elapsed between the original compact and the actual work. The second contract got eight rail sections capable of holding boats 350 feet in length and was completed in March 1854.[39]

No discussion of Paducah before the Civil War would be complete without mentioning the coming of the railroads. In 1850, Congress made grants of public land in Illinois to the Illinois Central Railroad to urge the completion of a railroad from Chicago to Cairo. At the same time, provision was made to complete the system from the Great Lakes to the Gulf by providing for the Mobile and Ohio (M&O), which was to terminate at some convenient place in western Kentucky to connect with the Illinois Central. It was accepted knowledge at the time that the southern line could not end opposite the mouth of the Ohio (where it now crosses just above the mouth over the Illinois Central Bridge at Cairo) on account of the large sandbar and a considerable amount of low land subject to flooding. Mounds, Illinois, came into being, hoping to be the terminus. Others in the race included the city of Paducah. Actually, Columbus won, and the line ended on the Mississippi, not the Ohio; however, rival terminals developed at both ends of the M&O.

New Orleans, not wishing to lose its premier position in trade to Mobile, encouraged the construction of a series of railroads that would connect the Queen City with the Illinois Central. Paducah saw an opportunity to link with both of these developing systems by joining on to the southern lines near Troy, Tennessee. The legislature, in its 1851–52 sessions, made it possible for Paducah to contribute to the stock of a railroad. The minutes of the meeting of the trustees on March 1, 1853, report that the town agreed to buy stock in the proposed railroad. The New Orleans and Ohio Railroad (NO&O) was to run sixty miles south from Paducah, and estimates were that the line would cost $1 million. Minutes of the council for March 25, 1853, include the ordinance authorizing the purchase of $200,000 in stock in the NO&O. Judge L.M. Flournoy; Judge James Campbell; John W. Crockett; S.F. Singleton; William Norton, chairman of the trustees; Henry Enders; James Langstaff; and B.F. Givens were among the promoters.

Lloyd Tilghman, member of a distinguished family from Maryland and a graduate of West Point, surveyed and supervised the construction of part of the road during the winter of 1853–54. By July 4, 1854, the road had progressed as far south as Florence (a distance of seven miles). The first train ran out of Paducah to Florence on Independence Day, and a barbecue was held to celebrate the event:

> *People drove in carriages and ox-teams and came on foot and horse and on mule-back from miles around to witness for the first time in their lives the thrilling spectacle of a roaring "iron horse" consuming wood and water and belching forth smoke, fire, and steam as it pulled a train of cars at the amazing speed of 15 miles per hour.*

This writer noted that the original equipment of the railroad consisted of a small, primitive engine "about as big as a thresher" and two small flat cars." Paducah was into the railroad era.[40]

Chapter 2

DISUNION

Between the founding of Paducah in 1830 and the start of the Civil War, criticism of slavery became more violent. In Kentucky, there were those who opposed the institution of slavery. Initially, it was hoped that slaves could be freed by purchase and returned to Africa. Henry Clay was among the founders of the colonization movement that contributed to the creation of Liberia in Africa; however, expense made this approach impractical. Other avenues were tried.

As early as 1808, the Kentucky Abolition Society spoke against slavery as being detrimental to humanity. Leaders of abolition included James Birney and Cassius Marcellus Clay; however, most Kentuckians were willing to abide the continued presence of slavery. Nevertheless, slavery was the central issue that led to the Constitution Convention of 1849 in Kentucky. Throughout that year, the state debated whether to call a convention. Slave owners were quite concerned about protecting their property. All resolutions were carefully examined to see if any suspicion of abolitionist sentiment could be detected. The convention met in October, and the delegates were overwhelmingly pro-slavery, even those from areas without slaves. Property in slaves was guaranteed by the new document. To further protect the institution from abolitionist taint, free Negroes were denied entry.

The year 1849 also saw the gold rush to California, accelerating the demand for a decision to be made regarding the disposition of the territory acquired from Mexico. It seemed as if the crisis would split the Union. The South was more adamant; the chance to gain political power was appealing.

The movement to resolve the crisis was led by Kentuckians—Henry Clay in the Senate and Linn Boyd in the House. The Compromise of 1850 managed to avert an open schism between slave and free states for another ten years. The most controversial of the eight sections of the compromise was the passage of a strong fugitive slave law that sought to assist owners to recover lost, strayed or stolen property in slaves. Perhaps, as a Kentucky slave owner remarked after chasing a fugitive into Ohio only to lose all trace of him, wayward slaves had found an underground railroad to freedom. The new law proposed to shut down this illegal operation.[41]

The new generation of politicians that replaced Webster, Clay, Boyd and Calhoun was not as willing to compromise. Attention shifted to Kansas and Nebraska. The prospect of a transcontinental railroad became more likely as people poured into California. Federal land grants to the Illinois Central in 1850 promised a precedent for future projects; however, the proposed route soon became the center of a power struggle between the slave states and the free-soil advocates. Obviously, Congress would not undertake more than one route. The possibility of the "ox-bow" route through Texas and the Mexican territory appealed to Southerners. Stephen A. Douglas of Illinois hoped to gain from the sale of property in Chicago if that city was one terminus; therefore, he solicited Southern support for the organization of Kansas and Nebraska into federal territories in order to open the central route through the Rockies for a railroad. In return for Southern support, Douglas agreed to support the position that the settlers in a region could decide for themselves on the issue of slavery at the time a territorial government was formed. Douglas called this position "popular sovereignty." If implemented, it meant that slavery could invade the territory excluded by the Missouri Compromise—a victory for Southern political aims.

One immediate result of the Kansas-Nebraska Act was the creation of two rival claimants to being the legal government of the Kansas territory. Violence was another consequence. One depredation begat another. The Whig Party began to split and lose identity. Only the Democratic Party remained to unite the nation because the new parties that emerged were sectional in outlook. The Republicans came into being in opposition to the Kansas-Nebraska Act. The first candidate of the new party was John C. Frémont in 1856. The basic tenets of the party were: high tariffs, free homesteads and no extension of slavery into the territories—none of which appealed to the South. Another new party was the Know-Nothing or American Party. This group was anti-foreign and anti-Catholic. James Buchanan, a Democrat known to lean toward the South despite being from Pennsylvania, was elected president. The issue of slavery was still not resolved.

Upon taking office, Buchanan asked the Supreme Court to settle the slavery question once and for all. The case used for this purpose was *Dred Scott v. Sandford*. The majority of the court was pro-Southern. As a result, slavery could not be excluded anywhere with the new ruling. The Missouri Compromise was declared unconstitutional. It appeared that the Southern drive for increased political power was winning.

The election of Abraham Lincoln in 1860 was a victory for the North and West. Since the party was sectional, the South felt it had nothing further to gain by remaining in the Union. Secession began.

What impact did these changing times have on Paducah? Like the rest of the nation, Paducahans followed events of the 1840s and 1850s with interest. It is difficult to relinquish beliefs acquired over years. The vast majority of the citizens of the Purchase were Democrats when that term meant pro-slave; however, Paducah, being on the river, came into contact with moderating influences. Among these must be noted the presence of a large number of Roman Catholics, who tended to moderate the more radical stand on slavery of the Baptists and Methodists (the former being the first to split over slavery in 1843, followed by the Methodists in 1844). A second element dedicated to moderation would be the Germans in general. After the turmoil that followed the European revolutions of 1848, these immigrants settled along the Ohio River in considerable numbers. Quickly, they became community leaders in Paducah. John Fisher became mayor in 1863 after twenty-five years in the bakery and brewery business. Others established in business included Ernest Rehkopf, William H. Rieke, Julius F. Wahl, Jacob Weil and Daniel Wolff.[42]

Paducah benefited from the diversity of denominations present in the town. Variety of religious worship moderated political and social beliefs. The Broadway Methodist Church was organized in 1834 by Reverends George W. Martin and George W. Cayce, and a church was built in 1842 by Kirby Jones. In the same year, the Presbyterian Church was organized on October 29 at the residence of James Campbell. The Baptists got their first building in 1842, having organized in 1839. The Episcopalians came in 1846 under the leadership of Reverend W.M. Cowgill. Three years later, the Christian Church was functioning under the leadership of Robert Rice. Father Elisha Durbin of Uniontown, Union County, served the first Catholic congregation, which was formed about 1848–49 at John Grief's residence. A Jewish cemetery was formed in 1863, and the

German Evangelical Church was established after the Civil War, as was the K.K. Yeshuron Jewish congregation.[43]

Paducah and McCracken County were anomalies in the voting pattern in the Purchase. Neither existed in the presidential election of 1824, when Calloway, Hickman and Graves Counties voted for Jackson in a losing effort. In 1828, over 80 percent of the voters in the Purchase voted for Jackson. This amount dropped slightly in 1832, when 79.8 percent of the voters in the Purchase supported the Democratic ticket. Beginning in 1836, a different pattern emerged. McCracken County alone in the Purchase supported Harrison and the new Whig Party. Of the 255 votes cast, 106, or 41.6 percent, went to Van Buren and 149, or 58.4 percent, were cast for Harrison. The same trend was evident in 1840. Only McCracken County voted Whig in the Purchase region, giving 59.5 percent of the vote to Harrison. Again in 1844, McCracken voted Whig, losing slightly in the total percentage of votes cast (56.8 percent). In fact, the total vote was down from 652 in 1840 to only 451 in 1844. Clay got 256 votes to 195 for the successful Polk. The Whigs kept their majority in McCracken in 1848. Of the 715 votes cast, the Whigs got 407, or 56.9 percent, thus helping put Zachary Taylor into the White House, even if for a short time (he died on July 9, 1850, and was succeeded by Millard Fillmore, who favored Clay and Boyd's compromise legislation). The election of 1852 saw McCracken voting Democratic; however, the vote cast was light. Franklin Pierce might have carried both McCracken and the country but without much enthusiasm. The following election, McCracken returned to its role as a maverick by turning to the Know-Nothing candidate rather than support the victorious Buchanan, giving 660 of 1,165 votes to Fillmore. In 1860, the bulk of voters in McCracken voted for the moderate John Bell (710). Douglas got 280; Breckinridge, the extreme Southern candidate, got 244; and Lincoln got 8.[44]

Paducah approached 1860 with confidence. The population of the town exceeded six thousand. It enjoyed the benefits of a railroad and had good river facilities, and the community was the focal point for wholesaling and retailing for an area that included Kentucky, southern Illinois, northern Tennessee and southeastern Missouri.

Chapter 3

KENTUCKY TRIES NEUTRALITY

Paducahans, like the majority of Kentuckians, did not wish to rush to war in 1860–61. R.B.J. Twyman was an avowed Democrat, yet the Paducah editor said:

> *When the telegraph announced that South Carolina had seceded from the Union, there were not half a dozen out-spoken secessionists in Paducah, but as State after State went out and took their stand by the side of South Carolina, the secession element gained strength, and one by one, the people turned over to the side of the Southern Confederacy. The Union party, however, maintained the ascendency in Paducah until the military forces of South Carolina fired upon Fort Sumter on April 14, 1861. As soon as the wires flashed the news of the surrender of this fortification throughout the country, the war was considered as having commenced, and all were wild with excitement. Men and women seemed really to go mad.*[45]

The fall of Fort Sumter prompted the president to issue a call for seventy-five thousand troops. On April 15, two days after the surrender of the fort, Simon Cameron, secretary of war, sent a telegram to Governor Beriah Magoffin asking for four regiments for "immediate service." On the same day, Magoffin sent a reply to Cameron declaring, "I say, emphatically, Kentucky will furnish no troops for the wicked purpose of subduing her sister Southern States." Two days later, in a public address at Lexington before a large audience, John J. Crittenden urged that Kentucky should take

Battle Lines of the Civil War. *Map by Ann Robertson, 1980.*

no part in the sectional strife but stand as a mediator for the North and South. On April 18, an immense crowd of Unionists met in Louisville and were addressed by James Guthrie, ex-senator Archibald Dixon and others; they passed resolutions reminding the State Guard that it had taken an oath to support both the United States and the government of Kentucky. This meeting produced a body known as the Union State Control Committee, composed of such men as James Speed and George D. Prentice, which made a strong endorsement of Magoffin's position and declared that Kentucky "ought to hold herself independent of both sides and compel both sides to respect the inviolability of her soil."[46]

The people within Columbus, Kentucky, were strong in their sentiments for the cause of the Confederacy, and as early as April 22, they sent a request to the Confederates to come and occupy them. B.W. Sharp, the mayor, was particularly partisan toward the South.[47] Gideon J. Pillow, charged with regulating the navigation of the Mississippi River for the Confederacy, determined to accede to the mayor's request.

McClellan heard of the proposed movement of Confederate troops into Kentucky, and on June 11, he sent the following dispatch to Governor Magoffin:

> *I have received information that Tennessee troops are under orders to occupy Island number one below Cairo. In accordance with my understanding with General Buckner, I call upon you to prevent this step. Do you regard the islands in the Mississippi River above the Tennessee line, as within your jurisdiction, and if so, what ones?*[48]

This telegram of McClellan's evoked the agreement with Buckner and seems to belie the later denial by McClellan of the existence of such an agreement. In any event, Governor Magoffin certainly thought such an agreement existed. So did Buckner, Lloyd Tilghman and Governor Harris of Tennessee.

Immediately upon receiving McClellan's telegram calling for action by Kentucky, Magoffin wired, "General Buckner has gone to Paducah and Columbus; his orders are to carry out his understanding with you. Am investigating the question of jurisdiction over the issue to which you allude."[49] On June 15, General Buckner gave specific orders to Colonel Lloyd Tilghman at Paducah to call into service six companies of the State Guard, four of infantry, one of artillery and one of cavalry. Upon formation, these units were to proceed, under the command of Colonel Tilghman, directly to Columbus to preserve the neutrality of the state at that point.[50]

Buckner soon found himself in an ambiguous position. He had sent Tilghman to Columbus in response to a request by a Federal officer, yet he was hampered in providing logistical support by another Federal agent. On June 25, Buckner arranged for a shipment of thirty tents and cooking utensils for 150 men from Louisville to Columbus. The surveyor of the port gave his approval, only to be countermanded by the Federal agent in charge of the port. As Buckner wrote to Scott Brown, adjutant general at Frankfort, W.P. Mellon seemed to claim the right under "the authority of the president to forbid the State of Kentucky from executing her laws, even when she is thereby discharging her duty to the general government."[51]

Buckner was not content to let the matter rest. He sent Alexander Casseday and George B. Johnson to the Galt House to see Mellon and try to persuade him to change his embargo on the supplies. Mellon refused. He said that the State Guard was disloyal, and he would not allow anything to be shipped to it, "whether it be a paper of needles, hogshead of meat, or camp kettles."[52]

Despite the impediment of Mellon, the threat of Confederate invasion abated for a time. Both North and South felt it expedient to respect Kentucky's neutrality for a while longer, but each sought to entice young men to enlist in their respective causes. The Third Kentucky was organized about July 29 by Lloyd Tilghman, who had turned the State Guard command over to Ben Hardin Helm, a brother-in-law of Lincoln. Soon, Tilghman was promoted to brigadier general.[53]

The defeat of the Federal army at the Battle of Bull Run (or the First Manassas, if one were Southern) on July 21, 1861, served to move Kentucky closer to declaring for the Union. Indeed, the next day, John J. Crittenden declared Kentucky for the Union. In August, immediately after the state elections returned a majority favoring the North, Camp Dick Robinson was established in Garrard County by Brigadier General William Nelson (late lieutenant of the navy). This was a direct violation of the state's neutrality, but the camp was tolerated, as the troops were moved out of the state as soon as they were organized. Frequently, recruits from the contending sides met in railroad stations—each preparing to depart from Kentucky to join in the fight.[54]

Thus far, both sides had refrained from active operations in Kentucky. A series of events in Missouri, Tennessee and Paducah proved to be the catalyst that brought Kentucky into the war.

Major General John. C. Frémont of the Union army commanded the Union forces in the Western Department with headquarters at St. Louis. If his abilities had equaled his ego, the war would have been over in a month; nevertheless, Frémont did realize that to make war in his department, the question of passing through Kentucky to reach the enemy must be resolved. To undertake action in this area, Frémont summoned the new commander at Cairo, Illinois, U.S. Grant, to headquarters at St. Louis. Frémont had intelligence that his counterpart Leonidas Polk (bishop of the Episcopal Church of Louisiana, graduate of West Point and an able officer) had been given command in Tennessee and was contemplating a move into Kentucky. Polk had the confidence of Jefferson Davis even if his recommendation meant violating the neutrality of Kentucky. High ground from which cannons could deny Union gunboats access to the Mississippi River proved to be more important than the sensibilities of Kentuckians.[55]

On August 20, 1861, a series of events in Paducah led directly to the entry of Kentucky into the war. The United States gunboat *Lexington* put a shot across the bow of the *W.B. Terry* in Paducah. R.N. Stembel, commander of the Union gunboat, reported the action to Colonel R.J. Oglesby at Cairo as justified. The *Terry* had been stopped, boarded, searched and seized. Stembel stated, "I had indisputable proof which examination of her papers found on board confirmed, that she was running in the employment of the Confederacy."[56] This action was reported to the area commander, Frémont, who, in turn, sent his report to General Lorenzo Thomas, adjutant general of the army: "Events had thus transpired clearly indicating the complicity of citizens of Kentucky with the rebel forces, and showing the impracticability of carrying on operation in that direction without involving Kentucky."[57]

The steamer *W.B. Terry* was owned jointly by three citizens of Paducah and one of Mississippi.[58] In retaliation for Stembel's action, Captain Johnson, late skipper of the *Terry*; A.M. Winston; White Fowler; and other Paducah citizens seized the boat *Samuel Orr*, the regular mail packet between Paducah and Evansville, Indiana. This small packet was quickly sent up the Tennessee River to Confederate territory.[59] After the war, owners of this craft sued to reclaim damages for the loss of the boat.

Lieutenant General Leonidas Polk heard of the two events—the appearance of Union forces opposite Columbus and the seizure of the *W.B. Terry*. Feeling that he could wait no longer for Kentucky to make up its mind, Polk sent a telegram to Governor Magoffin of Kentucky indicating Polk's intention to occupy Columbus:[60] "I think it is of the greatest consequence to the Southern cause in Kentucky or elsewhere that I should be ahead of the enemy in occupying Columbus and Paducah." Accordingly, on September 3, 1861, General Pillow led the vanguard of the Confederate army into Hickman while General Polk occupied Columbus with a force numbering between 1,500 and 2,000 men.[61]

Ulysses S. Grant now commanded the Federal forces at Cairo. The day after he took command from Richard Oglesby, word came to Grant from a scout who reported that Polk had moved into Kentucky. Grant sent word to Frémont via a messenger stating that unless he received orders to the contrary, he would occupy Paducah.[62] Then Grant embarked the Ninth and Twelfth Illinois and a four-gun battery of artillery on transports and waited for dawn on the sixth.[63]

Confederate flags were flying in Paducah in anticipation of the imminent arrival of the Southern troops, who were expected about noon, according to common report. The appearance of blue uniforms in this town offended many whose sympathies were ardently Southern. The Union assumption that all Paducahans were pro-Rebel was not conducive to improving relations between the invading force and the townsfolk. However, the presence of so many "plump, small-boned women" more than made up for the jeers and defiant cries the troops heard, and they "fell in love with Paducah on sight," as one soldier wrote.[64]

PROCLAMATION,

TO THE CITIZENS OF

PADUCAH!

I have come among you, not as an enemy, but as your friend and fellow-citizen, not to injure or annoy you, but to respect the rights, and to defend and enforce the rights of all loyal citizens. An enemy, in rebellion against our common Government, has taken possession of, and planted its guns upon the soil of Kentucky and fired upon our flag. Hickman and Columbus are in his hands. He is moving upon your city. I am here to defend you against this enemy and to assert and maintain the authority and sovereignty of your Government and mine. I have nothing to do with opinions. I shall deal only with armed rebellion and its aiders and abetors. Yon cau pursue your usual avocations without fear or hindrance. The strong arm of the Government is here to protect its friends, and to punish only its enemies. Whenever it is manifest that you are able to defend yourselves, to maintain the authority of your Government and protect the rights of all its loyal citizens, I shall withdraw the forces under my command from your city.

U. S. GRANT,

Brig. Gen. U. S. A., Commanding.

Paducah, Sept 6th. 1861

KENTUCKY'S 175TH ANNIVERSARY
1792 — 1967

SOUVENIR OF PADUCAH, KY.

General U.S. Grant's introduction to Paducah, September 6, 1861. Souvenir of Paducah on Kentucky's 175th anniversary, 1967.

Grant wrote that "when the National troops entered the town the citizens were taken by surprise. I never after saw such consternation depicted on the faces of the people." This surprise was reflected on sleepy faces: "Men, women, and children came out of their doors looking pale and frightened at the presence of the invader. They were expecting rebel troops that day." According to Grant, the Rebels had nearly four thousand men from Columbus and "were at that time within ten or fifteen miles of Paducah on their way to occupy the place." Actually, Frank Cheatham did have a small group near Mayfield and was proceeding toward Paducah when he heard of Grant's move.[65]

Once ashore, Grant moved fast. He had to. As he recalled, "I had but two regiments and one battery with me; but the enemy did not know this and returned to Columbus. I stationed my troops at the best points to guard the roads leading into the city, left gunboats to guard the river front and by noon was ready to start on my return to Cairo."[66]

Grant tried to assuage the populace:

> *Before leaving, however, I addressed a short printed proclamation to the citizens of Paducah assuring them of our peaceful intentions, that we had come among them to protect them against the enemies of our country, and that all who chose could continue their usual avocations with assurance of the protection of the government.*

Grant felt this assurance was effective; however, he did note that "the majority would have much preferred the presence of the other army."[67]

Grant's first act upon entering the city was to seize the railroad, the Federal marine hospital and the telegraph office and to send patrols out to block the roads. He also seized a quantity of supplies, including two tons of leather destined for the South and other contraband goods. He left strict orders for the deportment of the troops to prevent their plundering the populace or aggravating them further than was absolutely necessary. Brigadier E.A. Paine of Illinois was placed in command. He and Paducah were destined to meet again, under less restraint on the part of Paine.[68]

Whereas Polk had felt it necessary to inform Governor Magoffin, who sympathized with the South, about the motives for occupying Columbus, Grant also sought to sooth the political affront to Kentucky occasioned by the move against Paducah by wiring the pro-Union Speaker of the House of Kentucky that the Southern forces had invaded Kentucky territory. Frémont reprimanded Grant for not going through proper channels.[69]

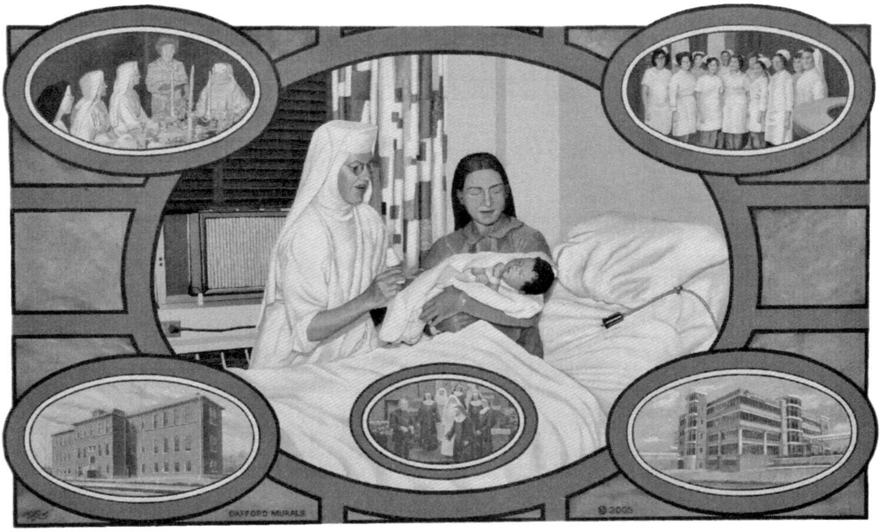

This Dafford mural celebrates hospital caregivers. Riverside City Hospital was erected on the site of the Marine Hospital (Fort Anderson). Later, the R.C. Diocese of Owensboro purchased Riverside in 1939, and the Sisters of St. Francis of Tiffin, Ohio, managed the renamed Lourdes. In 1973, Lourdes moved to the present location on Lone Oak Road. In 1991, the Sisters of Mercy became sponsors. Now the hospital is part of the Catholic Health Partners. The Marshall Nemer Pavilion was added in 2004.

Grant was not the only field commander to be criticized for the move into Kentucky. Polk's action also caused official correspondence to fly. Governor Harris of Tennessee sent President Davis a letter on September 4 in which Harris protested the move of Polk. The governor felt that he had pledged the support of his state in maintaining the neutrality of Kentucky and feared that Polk's action would harm the Southern cause. Harris asked Davis if "it would not be well to order their immediate withdrawal."[70]

President Davis had to face the problem of either offending Harris or showing a lack of support for his old friend and general. On September 13, Davis wrote to Polk, telling him to let the necessity of the move determine his actions.[71] It is surprising to note that on the same day, L.P. Walker, the Confederate secretary of war, wrote to Governor Harris that Polk had been ordered to withdraw.[72] Polk stood his ground. He stated that the occupation of the high ground at Columbus was an absolute necessity to be able to hold the state of Tennessee and other parts of the Confederacy. Polk held that it would be unwise to withdraw unless the Federal troops did likewise. Davis sustained Polk, disregarding Walker's orders.[73]

Polk had replied to the protests of both Governor Magoffin and John M. Johnson, chairman of a special committee of the Kentucky Senate. To Magoffin, Polk stressed that he had "reliable information that the Federal troops had in mind taking Columbus." Polk pointed out that the Confederate position in the west would be untenable without Columbus neutralized. He agreed to withdraw his troops if the Federal troops left.[74]

To Johnson, Polk was just as resolute. He responded to the senate resolution of September 9 as he had to Magoffin, adding that "we are not here by choice but by necessity."[75]

Grant had temporarily left General E.A. Paine in charge at Paducah. On September 6, Grant came with reinforcements. He marched his troops to a point on the Illinois shore opposite Paducah and waited until the engineers built a pontoon bridge across the Ohio. Approximately 123 forty-foot barges were used to span the river. At 3:30 p.m., the work was complete, and a band led the troops across the river to the tune of "Union Forever." A storm soon destroyed the bridge, but Paducah was secure by that time.[76]

On September 14, 1861, Paine was relieved of command by Charles F. Smith. This officer had been the commandant of the cadets at West Point when Grant arrived to study there. Smith was regular army and soon had the garrison at Paducah in top condition. In fact, Grant made it a rule to send Smith the better-trained soldiers and keep the recruits at Cairo under his own supervision.[77]

It appeared that Paducah would soon be the staging point for a major offensive against the South. Grant was a fighter. No one would fault him on that. The Confederates had established a line in Kentucky running from Columbus in the west to Bowling Green, where Simon Bolivar Buckner commanded, to the Cumberland Gap, where Felix Zollicoffer held the passes. To counter this wall of defense, Grant built Fort Holt and Fort Jefferson near Wickliffe and Fort Anderson at Paducah to protect the Tennessee and Cumberland Rivers.

On September 8, 1861, Colonel G. Waagner boarded the ironclad *Lexington* at Cairo and set off for a reconnaissance down the Mississippi to Lucas Bend, just north of Columbus. Guns from the works at Columbus engaged the boat at extreme range, with little effect. The Confederates fired twenty-four-pound howitzers, twenty-four- and thirty-two-pounders on barbette carriages. All fell short due to weak powder and fuses that were cut too long. When two Confederate boats set out in pursuit, the *Lexington* retired.[78] Still, Grant was wishing for more specific information concerning the intentions of the enemy in Kentucky.

September 10 saw several events of importance to Paducah and the Purchase region. On that date, Albert Sidney Johnston, a Kentuckian, had superseded General Polk as commander of Department No. 2, with Polk keeping the command at Columbus and the defense of the entire Mississippi River below Cairo.[79] Also on this day, another party scouted the area near Lucas Bend. This time some damage was done to both sides. The *Yankee*, a Confederate boat—obviously misnamed—was disabled, and the *Conestoga* of the Union had one man wounded.[80]

Grant and Polk reacted differently to reports of this skirmish. Grant kept pestering Frémont for permission to attack the works of Columbus. Polk called for additional troops for defense.

Grant reported to Frémont on September 10 that the Confederates were sending troops across the river to Belmont, Missouri. At that time, the Federals thought that the Rebels had about fifteen pieces of artillery on wheels and one large cannon in position at Belmont.[81] Grant also reported the exchange of shots at Lucas Bend and noted that he felt this action was good for morale, adding, "With a little addition to my present force I would take Columbus."[82] The following day, Grant instructed Colonel Oglesby, commanding at Norfolk, Missouri, to keep up the reconnaissance and keep "annoying the enemy in every way possible."[83] On the twelfth, Grant wrote to Frémont that he was

> *of the opinion that if a demonstration was made from Paducah toward Union City supported by two columns on the Kentucky side from here, the gunboats, and a force moving upon Belmont, the enemy would be forced to leave Columbus, leaving behind their heavy ordnance. I submit this to your consideration, and will hold myself in readiness to execute this or any plan you may adopt.*[84]

Had it not been for a sudden defeat of the Union forces in Missouri, Frémont might have gone along with Grant's plan to attack Columbus. The idea was similar to one Frémont had presented to Lincoln for a grand movement into the South. Frémont did order Grant to scout the roads to Columbus and to meet the enemy at Belmont, if necessary.[85]

Grant wrote to Smith at Paducah on September 20 that he had lost two regiments that were sent to the defense of Washington. Grant complained that he had "scarcely more than a weak garrison."[86] In addition, Grant ordered Oglesby to withdraw from the outpost at Norfolk to Bird's Point on October l. As Grant told Oglesby, he was "despairing of being reinforced. I deem it the better part of valor to be prudent."[87]

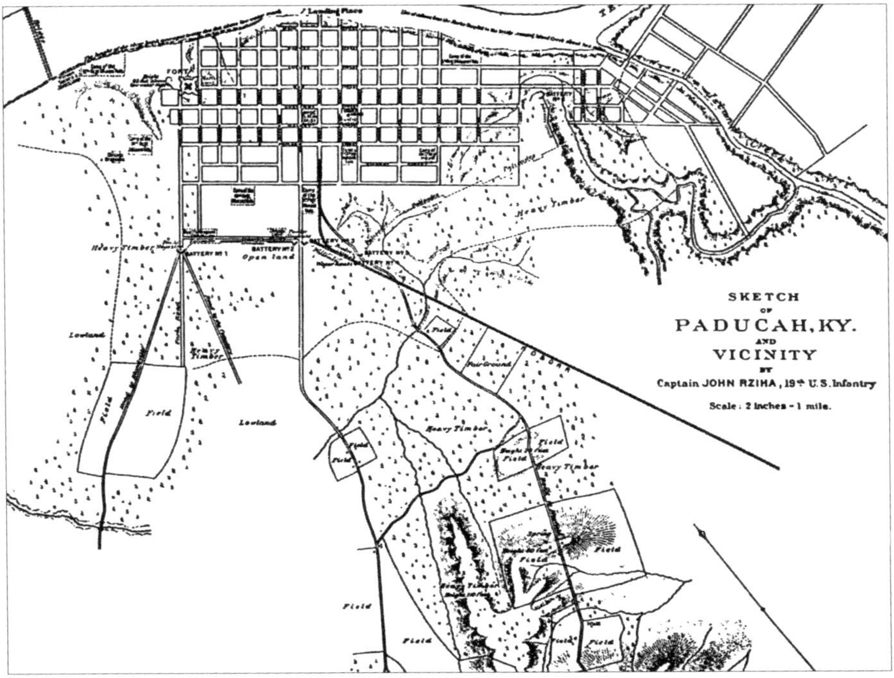

Sketch of Paducah, Kentucky, in *Official Records of the War of the Rebellion*, Series I, Vol. 4.

On November 5, Grant received a report that the Confederates at Columbus were sending troops in strength as reinforcements to Price.[88] Immediately, Grant ordered all remaining troops under his command at Cairo, Bird's Point and Fort Holt on the Kentucky side to make plans for a demonstration against Columbus. Orders were also sent to General Smith, commanding at Paducah, to make a similar demonstration on the Kentucky side of the river toward Columbus but not to go nearer than ten or twelve miles.[89] The purpose of this maneuvering was to make Polk think he was under attack, causing him to recall the support he had given Price; thus, Grant prevented the possibility of the Rebels cutting off two small Union columns of Oglesby's and Plummer's by troops that had crossed from Columbus the day before.[90]

Grant was fully aware of the strength of the Confederate works at Columbus. He had requested orders on several occasions to move on Columbus during September, but the position had been strengthened to such an extent that it could be reduced only by a long siege. With conditions as they were on this November day, Grant sought only to protect his columns moving against Price and to give his men at Cairo and Paducah a taste of powder.[91]

During the evening of November 6, Grant started down the Mississippi from Cairo with about three thousand men of five regiments of infantry, two guns and two companies of cavalry. He landed on the Kentucky shore ten miles above Columbus to put out pickets and to contact the troops from Paducah under General Smith. This was the closest his army had been to action thus far, and the entire command was elated at the prospect. Grant felt he could not maintain discipline much longer without some chance for action, so he determined to change the operation from a demonstration to a raid. Smith would keep the attention of the fort at Columbus while Grant landed on the Missouri shore and attacked the outpost at Belmont.[92]

The Battle of Belmont is frequently given short attention in studies of the Civil War. This raid accomplished its purpose in that Grant cut through the enemy defensive line and took Belmont. The battle might be considered a Confederate victory in that the Rebels occupied the field and suffered fewer casualties. Grant's command had to fight all the way to the transports as reinforcements from Columbus crossed the river during the fighting and almost cut off the Union forces. What is frequently overlooked is how close the South came to winning the war in this battle. Grant nearly lost his life on three occasions. One time, he faced the entire Confederate army alone, and no one shot at him. Again, he was the last to board the transports—a feat he could not have managed in time to avoid death or capture had it not been for his horse sliding down a single plank to the deck of the boat as it left shore. Finally, Grant flung himself on a couch in the captain's cabin adjoining the pilothouse: "I did not keep that position a moment, but rose to go out on the deck to observe what was going on. I had scarcely left the sofa when a musket ball entered the room, struck the head of the sofa, passed through it and lodged in the foot."[93] Without Grant, it is doubtful that the Union would have won the war. The daring of Grant in the West turned the tide to the Union, and Grant's determination to break the Army of Northern Virginia led to victory in the East.

On the Kentucky shore, events were less hectic. General Smith did as Grant expected. One of Smith's officers let the enthusiasm generated by the sound of firing get the better of him, and he advanced beyond the limit set by Grant. This breach of discipline so incensed Smith that he demanded a court-martial for E.A. Paine. Smith charged Paine with having "a fixed purpose from the start to gain notoriety without reference to the public service or his plain duty as a soldier." Paine was to cause the citizens of Paducah even more anxiety than he did old C.F. Smith. In fact, Paine became the nemesis of the town, offending Jews, merchants, mayors and masses before he was finished.[94]

Occupation of Paducah by Union forces led to friction that deepened as time passed. Paducahans did not hesitate to show their displeasure at the presence of the Federals. Officers occupied private houses; some businesses, such as the bakery of George Oehlschlaeger and the gun shop of Ferd Hummel, were practically commandeered for the use of the army. Nevertheless, the town remained relatively quiet in 1862 except for a conspiracy started by General Paine to oust Smith.[95]

Paducah was not accustomed to the parade ground discipline insisted on by C.F. Smith. "His own men had not caught on to him yet, and his insistence on drill, on the use of spade and ax to build fortifications, and on the precise observation of what the book said enlisted men ought to do, seemed unfeeling and harsh." Others did not understand Smith's letter-of-the-law approach to Rebels and their sympathizers.[96]

Henry Wager Halleck, "Old Brains," replaced Frémont at St. Louis. Not long after Smith had reprimanded Paine after the Battle of Belmont, a letter from an irate citizen at Paducah accused Smith of being "soft" on Rebels. The writer felt that Smith should confiscate provisions and materials going to Rebel sympathizers instead of observing the contraband laws and confiscating only such material destined for the Rebel army. The letter also complained that Smith protects "rebels whilst union men suffer—and the soldiers [are] ready to rise against his policy."[97]

Early in 1863, Grant started the campaign that eventually cost the South the Mississippi and perhaps the war. The first objective was the poorly constructed fort on the Tennessee River near the border between Kentucky and Tennessee. Fort Henry was commanded by General Lloyd Tilghman of Paducah. He had sense enough to realize that the post was not defensible; therefore, he sent his soldiers across to Fort Donelson on the Cumberland near Dover. Tilghman planned only a token defense against the Union gunboats. On February 6, the post fell to the Union ironclads of Andrew Foote. The victorious gunboats came back to Paducah en route to the Cumberland and Donelson.[98]

February 12 to 16 saw the Union forces surround and take Fort Donelson. There were three Confederate brigadiers present: John Floyd of Virginia; Gideon J. Pillow of Columbia, Tennessee; and Simon Bolivar Buckner of Kentucky. Floyd had been secretary of war under former president Buchanan and feared he would be hanged for treason if captured. So he left. Pillow also left without comment. Buckner was left holding the post and had to send a delegation to Grant asking for terms of surrender. Grant, thinking Pillow was in command, gave the most insulting terms he could think of: unconditional surrender. Buckner was forced to accept. Ironically, when Grant left the regular army for drinking and arrived in New York, broke and wanting to go back to his father's place in Galena, he met an old friend from West Point who loaned him enough money to get to his family home to Illinois. That old friend was Buckner.

The fall of Forts Henry and Donelson opened the vitals of the Confederacy to penetration by Union ironclads. The Tennessee was open as far as Muscle Shoals, Alabama. Nashville lay on the Cumberland. In a short time, the general line of battle had moved out of Kentucky. Bowling Green and Columbus were abandoned without a fight, being outflanked by Grant. Nashville fell. The war entered a new phase.[99]

With the threat of military action removed from the immediate vicinity of Paducah, that town settled down to a more routine life. The city became a staging area for operations farther south. On April 2, 1862, considerable damage was done by wind. Seventeen stores, hotels and other structures were damaged, including the spire of the Methodist church.[100]

Four days later, the first massive battle in the West took place at Pittsburgh Landing, or Shiloh. Grant managed to stop the Confederates. Albert Sidney Johnston bled to death from what should have been a minor wound, and Grant lost his naïve hope of a quick victory over the South. War became hell. There was no longer tolerance for dissent.

Following the Battle of Shiloh, Paducah became a vast hospital for sick and wounded soldiers. "The Presbyterian, Baptist, Episcopal, Christian, and Methodist Churches, the Female Seminary, the court house, and other public and private buildings were taken possession of for such purposes, and some of them continued to be used thus till the close of the war."[101]

In order to cope with Confederate raids into parts of Kentucky, such as the forays of John Hunt Morgan in 1862 and 1864 and Nathan Bedford Forrest's two raids in 1864, martial law was declared in the state on July 31, 1863, on the orders of Ambrose Burnside. This action was taken "for the purpose only of protecting the rights of loyal citizens and the freedom of election." In practice, no disloyal person could vote. The power of decision rested with the army. Federal officials also limited the amount of material that a merchant in an exposed area might have on hand to prevent that sector from becoming a prime target for raiders. To this end, Federal treasury agents gauged the amount of merchandise of all kinds to be allowed in certain towns, and no merchant was permitted more than two months' supply of goods and material on hand at any given time.[102] This proved especially galling to wholesale merchants such as those in Paducah.

On April 29, 1865, all restrictions on trade east of the Mississippi were removed (except contraband of war), and on June 24, this order was extended to include the region west of the Mississippi. Not until August 29 was the last restriction of trade removed and the country a single unit again in trade on inland waters.[103]

Chapter 4
THE REIGN OF TERROR

Among the first to feel persecution from the military were the Jews. The role of the Jew in Paducah differs from that in many other cities. Not only have the Germans and Jews from Germany formed a welcomed part of the leadership in the business community of the town from very early times, but also one of the mayors serving the longest span in that office in Paducah was a German Jew, Meyer Weil (four terms, 1871, 1873, 1875 and 1877). Weil came to Paducah in 1863 and set up in the tobacco and brokerage business. Perhaps the reaction to Yankee persecution helped foster the sympathetic attitude toward Paducah Jews. General Order No. 11, issued by Grant on December 17, 1862, at Holly Springs, is a milestone in anti-Semitism by an agent of the government of the United States. It stated:

> *The Jews, as a class violating every regulation of trade established by the Treasury Department and also department orders, are hereby expelled from the department within twenty-four hours from receipt of this order.*
>
> *Post commanders will see that all of this class of people be furnished passes and required to leave and any one returning after such notification will be arrested and held in confinement until an opportunity occurs of sending them out as prisoners, unless furnished with permit from headquarters.*
>
> *No passes will be given these people to visit headquarters for the purpose of making personal application for trade permits.*[104]

Among those sent to Cincinnati from Paducah were J.W. Kaskel, D. Wolff and Caesar Kaskel. An appeal was made to "Father Abraham" via Congressman John A. Gurley of Ohio, and Lincoln had the order rescinded.[105]

General Halleck told Grant the reason Lincoln overruled his order:

> *The President has no objection to your expelling traitors and Jew peddlers, which, suppose, was the object of your order; but, as it is terms proscribed an entire religious class, some of whom are fighting in our ranks, the President deemed it necessary to revoke it.*[106]

Among the Jewish community in Paducah today there is a tradition that tells how Jews were hidden by citizens of Paducah to prevent their being sent to army camps. One soldier is said to have knocked on the door of a Jew and demanded, "What are you?" Not having a good command of the language, the Jew replied, "Tailor." Then the soldier said, "Sorry to bother you, Mr. Taylor, but I'm looking for Jews."[107]

Usurpation of states' rights caused friction between Federal and state officials in Kentucky. The commonwealth might have declared for the Union, but it continued to send men and supplies to the Confederacy. Furthermore, the state jealously protected property in slaves until all alternatives had been exhausted. Kentucky was equally protective of its prerogatives as a sovereign state in a union of states.

During 1862, efforts were made by Federal officials to ensure the election of those sympathetic with Union objectives. On July 21 at Louisville, General Jerry Boyle issued General Order No. 5: "No person hostile in opinion to the government and desiring its overthrow will be allowed to stand for office in the district of Kentucky."[108] Helped by this order, R.K. Williams of Paducah was elected to the Court of Appeals for the Fourth District; however, other candidates did not fare as well.[109]

Governor Magoffin detailed election irregularities in his report to the legislature issued on August 15, 1862. Documents 1 to 9 embrace the correspondence between circuit judge Wiley P. Fowler of Smithland, county judge G.A. Flournoy and county clerk Thomas D. Grundy of McCracken County and Colonel S. Noble, commanding the United States Army at Paducah. The governor detailed the gross disregard of the rights of state officials by the military. At issue was an oath. Noble wrote to Fowler, "Officers of your court in different counties are secessionists, and have not taken the oath of allegiance." He further claimed that these same men were "oppressing Union men, and talking treason in the very presence of the court." Noble lectured Fowler by pointing out that "the Union army came here to sustain and defend the constitution of the United States, to protect Union men, and punish treason wherever it may be found, whether in high or low places." To comply with the regulations, Fowler had to ensure that all jurors, both grand and petit, should take the oath before being impaneled. Noble concluded, "I want a record of such oath sent to these headquarters."[110]

Fowler "refused to comply with the order, declined to yield to any dictation by military authority as to the discharge of his duties as presiding officer of the court, and ordered an immediate adjournment until court in course."[111] Magoffin concurred with the conduct of Fowler on May 20: "For the dignity of the bench, for the honor of the state, in the name of the liberties of our people, I hope you will pay no attention to the illegal, unconstitutional, and tyrannical action."[112] In fact, Magoffin advised Fowler not to appear as ordered at Paducah. Fowler did appear on May 23.

Noble also held Flournoy and Grundy to the same oath requirement. They told the colonel that they had taken all the oaths necessary and required by the laws of Kentucky. They were denied the exercise of their offices.[113] Magoffin protested this action to John J. Crittenden in Washington, and Crittenden took up the matter with the secretary of war. On June 7, Crittenden was informed that General Halleck would "investigate and report."[114] Nothing came of this.

The tenth document Magoffin sent to the legislature was a letter from J. Bigger of Paducah dated July 8, 1862. Bigger complained that the military had denied him the right to hold office under the Kentucky Constitution:

> *On this morning an order was presented to me purporting to have been issued from the office of the provost marshal at this place, by command of Brig. Gen. Boyle, directing me to decline the office of circuit judge of the first judicial district; and upon my failure to comply, I am informed that I will be reported under arrest to headquarters United States forces at Louisville, Ky.*[115]

Bigger noted that he had the necessary qualifications for the position under state law.

Intervention in elections by the military was unnecessary. From the entry of Kentucky into the war, the legislature had passed several measures dealing with Rebels and their supporters.[116] Still, the military felt that the state did not do enough. Kentucky might have been legally correct, but such precise behavior was not enough. As time passed, the goal of the military was to punish those who gave aid and comfort to the South.

The year 1864 proved to be a dramatic one for Paducah. Interference in both the political and economic life of the community by the Federal officials offended Paducahans. Gradually, the moderate element became more and more disenchanted with their treatment. The city became more partisan toward the South. If Paducahans had been disturbed by the army's interference before, they had even greater cause for alarm in 1864. In that year, three crises confronted the townspeople: the Federal authorities openly attacked the institution of slavery by recruiting Kentucky Negroes into the military, a Confederate raid by Nathan Bedford Forrest caused some physical damage and encouraged deeper sentiment for the South and a ruthless purge of anti-Unionists by General E.A. Paine deeply distressed Paducahans.

Union recruiters began to enroll Negroes despite the opposition of Kentuckians. On July 8, 1863, the United States War Department authorized the enlistment of free Negroes into the armed forces. Kentuckians objected to this innovation so strongly that Lincoln lifted the application to Kentucky on October 25; however, by 1864, the situation had changed. The Union determined to recruit slaves in Kentucky on February 27. Lorenzo Thomas telegraphed Stanton: "I arrived here this morning. In my letter of the 1st instant, I reported instructions respecting the First Artillery Regiment Colored Troops, to be raised at Paducah, Kentucky. Shall I proceed with its organization?"[117] By the end of the war, two black artillery regiments and parts of several black infantry regiments had been recruited at Paducah.

Enlistment in the armed forces freed a slave and his family. Enlistment also meant a high risk since soldiers in the black units had exceedingly high death rates. If captured, the risks were even greater. Some were sold into slavery; others were killed. "In 1864 a Confederate officer, Col. W.P. Shingler, told his subordinates not to report the capture of any more Negroes."[118]

The use of Negroes as soldiers was not popular in Kentucky, especially in Paducah, where they were stationed. On March 21, 1864, Colonel Richard L. Cunningham of the Eighth U.S. Heavy Artillery (Colored) sent some of his black soldiers at Paducah to recruit Negro deck hands off the steamer *Carrie Jacobs*. The officers and crew of the boat resisted and appealed to white soldiers nearby for help. A fight ensued between blacks and whites, and several on each side were reported seriously injured.[119] This incident was indicative of the deep division that existed over the use of blacks as soldiers. There was no similar incident when whites were recruited for the Union at Paducah.

George F. Barnes started recruiting whites for the Sixteenth Kentucky Cavalry on February 15, 1864. Barnes was assisted by John E. Williamson,

E.J. Pendrick, H.H. Hamilton and S.B. McAfee (later, this outfit became part of the Twelfth Cavalry).[120] The unit was still raw and untried when it was called on to help defend Paducah against attack by other Paducahans in the second crisis of 1864.

Nathan Bedford Forrest sent Abraham Buford's Kentuckians (including many from the Purchase area) north toward Paducah in an attempt to relieve hard-pressed Confederate forces fighting before Atlanta. The goal of the raid was to cut the vital supply lines running through Kentucky. Captain H.A. Taylor led the advance with his company of the 12th Kentucky, CSA. Federal pickets were encountered three or four miles from the city of Paducah and were pushed in on their fortifications. The Federal force, led by Colonel S.G. Hicks of Illinois, consisted of the 122nd Illinois Infantry, 16th Kentucky Cavalry and 1st Kentucky Artillery, as well as the 8th U.S. Heavy Artillery (Colored). The Federals withdrew into Fort Anderson, where they were supported by fire from the gunboats *Peosta* and *Paw-Paw*.[121]

As soon as the Confederates came within cannon shot, the guns in the fort opened up on them. A participant recalled that "the Kentuckians were dismounted and moved in line of battle in the direction of the fort. The alignment was maintained until the more densely built-up portion of the city was reached, when it was broken by the buildings and the further advance had to be made along the streets in column by regiments or companies." The Confederates halted for a short time about three hundred yards from the enemy and protected themselves by getting behind houses in the streets and alleys that ran at right angles to those leading out in the direction of the fort.

> *While marching through the streets the command was under a constant and withering fire from the fort by both small arms and artillery. When out in the open space, the lines were somewhat adjusted before the final charge was made. When within a short distance of the fort it was discovered that it was surrounded by a deep ditch with such perpendicular banks as to render crossing impossible.*

At that, a retreat was ordered back to the cover of the buildings. There, "a terrific fire was kept up on the fort until near night, at which time the whole command was withdrawn a short distance from the city and went into camp for the night."[122]

Forrest is generally considered to be one of the most effective leaders on either side in the war. However, the attack on Fort Anderson does little to enhance his reputation. Perhaps Forrest counted too much on the lack of training of the Federals; perhaps he acceded too quickly to the demands of the Paducah personnel, who wanted to impress the home folks; or perhaps he felt that sheer audacity would carry the day. For whatever reason, Forrest did not make a proper reconnaissance. The ditch should not have been a surprise. Of this engagement, Forrest said, "I drove the enemy to their gunboats and fort, and held the town for ten hours; captured many stores and horses; burned sixty bales of cotton, one steamer and a dry dock, bringing out fifty prisoners. My loss, as far as known, is twenty-five killed and wounded, among them Colonel Thompson."[123] A.P. Thompson had been given command of the brigade to allow him the honor of taking his hometown. He was killed instantly by a cannonball while leading his troops in the approach to the fort. Colonel Edward Crossland took over only to be seriously wounded. The Union losses were fourteen killed, forty-six wounded and forty prisoners.[124]

Forrest moved back to Mayfield the morning after the raid, and the Kentuckians in his command disbanded for a few days so that they might visit their homes. It is to their everlasting credit to note that they did not abuse this first opportunity since 1861 to see kith and kin. All returned to their command at the appointed time. The Kentuckians made the most of their short visit. They procured good mounts and comfortable clothing and gathered up a number of fresh recruits, which brought the regiments up to something like their proper size again.[125]

Paducah suffered considerable damage, both by the raiders in their deliberate destruction of military stores and by the defenders in their efforts to defend the fort. The Union headquarters, quartermaster and the commissary buildings with all stores; the steamboat *Dacotah*; and the railroad depot were put to the torch. The defenders burned all the houses near the fort to prevent their being used again to shelter an attacking party.[126]

Forrest was not finished in the Purchase. He unsuccessfully attacked Fort Anderson (with its Negro defenders as one possible target), but another opportunity soon presented itself to impress on the blacks the folly of taking up arms against the Confederacy. This was the massacre at Fort Pillow, Tennessee, where the Union garrison surrendered only to have the black troops shot, driven into the Mississippi or buried alive in one or two instances. Had Fort Anderson capitulated, the same fate would have awaited the Negro contingent of the Union garrison at Paducah. "Forrest at Paducah…in weeks immediately preceding had indicated that if he must storm the works 'no quarter' would be shown the Negro troops." Forrest felt Negroes were property, not people.[127]

The vacationing Kentuckians of Forrest's command came together at Trenton, Tennessee, by the first part of April 1864. Forrest ordered General Buford to take them back into western Kentucky for two purposes: "First, to direct the attention of the Federal commanders away from Fort Pillow, which Forrest planned to take; secondly, to capture a lot of good horses and mules that were reported to be in the suburbs of Paducah."[128]

Buford sent Captain H.A. Tayler with about 110 men to make a demonstration before Columbus to pin the garrison in the fortifications while the main body raided Paducah. Tayler was so successful that the Union commander at Columbus thought he was under attack by Forrest's complete command. Buford arrived at Paducah on the morning of the fourteenth and made a great flurry of movement, driving the pickets back into the fort and onto the gunboats. The Union garrison remained pinned down by a few men while Buford's men gathered up about two hundred animals that had been overlooked during their first visit. After procuring the horses, Buford leisurely moved his command back to Trenton, giving some men additional furloughs on the way.[129]

Popular support of Forrest during the two raids caused Union commanders to demand harsher measures to suppress Southern sentiment. Prior to Forrest's raid in 1864, the Treasury Department had removed all restrictions on trade in Kentucky and Missouri. Immediately after the Confederate incursion, the Federal commander at Cairo complained to General Grant that "goods going from Cairo, Paducah, and Hickman will undoubtedly reach Tennessee if unrestricted, as I have not sufficient force to guard the whole border."[130] This soon proved to be the state of affairs. Federal officials claimed that the railroad from Paducah to Mayfield and from Columbus to Union City, Tennessee, was used to transport goods to the Confederacy—especially to the cavalry of Forrest, who was still in the region.[131] The commander at Cairo said that "for the past few months the interior of Western Kentucky has been filled with war-like stores and army supplies of every kind." He blamed the situation on "the loose administration of the Treasury and Army officials."[132]

The Federal commander at Cairo finally acted on his own initiative. On April 2, he issued a general order forbidding steamboats from landing between Paducah and Memphis. In addition, he halted the use of all ferryboats, trading boats, skiffs or other small craft operating on the Ohio and Mississippi Rivers in this area. All traffic out of Paducah and Columbus was prohibited except for military purposes.[133] The treasury approved this action on April 13. However, not all complaints came from the army. A group of Paducah merchants calling themselves the Union League of America protested that the "rebels are doing all the business, and they are reaping all the advantages of trade."[134]

The two raids by Forrest in March through western Kentucky and the sweeps through the center of the state by Morgan during the first part of June heartened the faltering Rebel supporters and caused an increase in guerrilla depredations. The ease and frequency of the incursions of Confederate regulars, coupled with the mounting boldness of the irregulars, caused General Elihu B. Washburne, commanding the District of West Tennessee, which included that part of Kentucky west of the Cumberland River, to issue an order that "the people of that disloyal region, Western Kentucky, will not be allowed to sell their cotton and tobacco, or purchase supplies, unless they show some friendship for the United States government, by driving out the guerrillas and irregular bands of Confederate soldiers who pay them frequent visits."[135]

On July 5, President Lincoln was so alarmed at the deterioration of the situation in Kentucky that he acted unilaterally. The writ of habeas corpus was suspended, and martial law was proclaimed.[136] From this date on, the fate of people suspected of supporting the South hinged on the caprices of military commanders. Eleven days later, General Order No. 59, of General Stephen Burbridge, provided that all Rebel sympathizers living within five miles of a guerrilla outrage should be arrested and deported beyond the limits of the United States, their property seized in sufficient quantity to repay losses arising from enemy action. For every unarmed Union citizen killed by guerrillas, four guerrilla prisoners should be taken from the nearest military prison and shot at a spot near the outrage.[137]

On July 19, 1864, E.A. Paine assumed command at Paducah and began a fifty-one-day reign of terror. Paine declared that only loyal people would be allowed to trade. To enforce this decision, he levied "a tax of $10 on every hogshead of tobacco or bale of cotton, and a tax assessment of 25 per cent ad valorum on all cotton which had ever been the property of a disloyal person."[138] On August 1, a tax of $100,000 was levied by Paine on residents of his military district to be collected from "persons known to be or suspected of being Confederate sympathizers."[139] In addition, "heavy sums were paid for [trade] permits, which, if admissible, should have been freely granted, and, if improper, should have...been refused."[140] These trade permits had been authorized by Burbridge's General Order No. 63 on August 13, which absolutely interdicted all shipments of produce or goods of any kind, either in, through or into the state—except upon a permit issued for four months to persons of "well known loyalty," whose status was determined "by a board of five advisors, well known citizens of unquestioned loyalty, respectability, and integrity, and who, in case of doubt, will be bound by an oath."[141] Should irregularities occur, the parties would be arrested and imprisoned, and their goods would be seized by the military.

Bank checks were not to pass unless they had the approval of Paine or one of his agents. The privilege of using bank drafts now cost fifty cents each. A standing charge of ten cents was made on all letters, newspapers or packages that left Paducah. In some instances, such as the case of black soldiers in the Union garrison, fifty cents was charged for permission to send letters to relatives.[142]

On August 8, 1864, Paine banished a group of citizens from Paducah to Canada. Among those from Paducah were Mrs. Robert Woolfolk and family (eight persons; Mr. Woolfolk had been banished two weeks earlier by Paine), Mrs. Hobbs, Mrs. Melrouse and sister and Robert Shanklin.[143]

John Sauner, who had been mayor from 1859 to 1863, had been called before General Paine and damned as a secessionist. Sauner said, "General, if I were on equal terms, you couldn't call me those names." Paine ordered the guard to shoot Sauner if he made any advance. He gave Sauner "a good cussing" for about an hour, ending with another threat to shoot the mayor if he got in the way. Sauner took the hint and left Paducah on the first boat for Cincinnati; he did not return until Paine had left.[144]

Despite the rigid censorship Paine exercised through the control of all mail leaving the city, word of the situation in Paducah got through to Jesse J. Craddock of the First Regiment of Capital Guards at Frankfort. Craddock sent a petition to General Burbridge. As a result, Brigadier General Speed Smith and Colonel John Mason Brown went to Paducah to conduct an investigation into Paine's conduct. Before the commission arrived, Paine fled to Illinois with all his records. The two officers found a mess. Citizens had been grossly abused, the least of which was the habitual salutation Paine gave to local inhabitants. At the slightest provocation, he would rage and shout, "You are a God-damned scoundrel; God-damn you. I'll dig a hole, shoot you, and put you in it."[145]

In its report, the commission furnished sworn testimony to the effect that Lucien Anderson, congressman of the First District; John F. Bollinger; R.H. Hall, provost marshal; Major Henry Bartling, Eighth U.S. Heavy Artillery (Colored); and Thomas M. Redd, surveyor of the port of Paducah, were involved in various acts of corruption, bribery, gross malfeasance and oppression of the population of Paducah. Others were also cited for acts equally shocking.[146]

The first act of Brigadier General S. Meredith upon assuming command at Paducah was to release fifty-one prisoners at Mayfield and to empty the guardhouse at Paducah.[147] The reign of terror was over; however, Kentuckians still were not secure. An exchange of letters between Governor Thomas Bramlette of Kentucky and President Lincoln, between Bramlette and General Burbridge and between Lincoln and Burbridge resulted. On January 8, 1865, Lincoln set aside the order of Burbridge that restricted all trade with Kentucky. Finally, to rid himself of the constant squabbles in Kentucky, Lincoln placed Major General John Palmer in command. Most Kentuckians agreed with the *Louisville Journal* and rejoiced, "Thank God and President Lincoln."[148]

Chapter 5

REUNION AND REBUILDING

The end of the Civil War found Paducah, like many other cities in Kentucky, facing the problem of reabsorbing that part of its population that had fought for either the South or the North and creating a place within the society for that part of the population that had been chattel. Patterns of commerce disrupted during the war had to be renewed and realigned. In the period following the depression of 1873, default and debt became a specter that haunted the city; still, Paducah weathered the series of crises and emerged strong and vibrant.

The end of the war did not mean the end of slavery in Kentucky. The commonwealth insisted on its right to maintain property in chattel up to the very end. Kentucky refused to ratify the Thirteenth Amendment, which ended the peculiar institution, and haughtily rejected any suggestion that the state should anticipate the inevitable and abolish slavery voluntarily. The Negro was freed by the Thirteenth Amendment, but he was not a citizen; rather, he was a ward of the federal government under the Freedman's Bureau. He could not testify in a state court against a white man, and he could not vote. Changes soon made both of these possible. Congress passed the Fourteenth Amendment on July 28, 1868, making the Negro a citizen without the support of Kentucky. The Fifteenth Amendment, ratified on March 30, 1870, gave the Negro the right to vote. Again, Kentucky opposed passage of the measure. Under the protection of the military, freedmen flocked to the cities. State laws did not apply to the freedmen. This pattern was perpetuated with the inclusion of Kentucky under the jurisdiction of the Freedman's Bureau in December 1865. An office opened at Paducah to oversee the transformation of the freedmen into citizens. Officials in Kentucky felt that their state should not have been included in the application of the Freedman's Bureau; nevertheless, all disputes involving Negroes now were heard in the bureau rather in the regular state tribunals.[149] Thus, the slave went from the protection of his master to the army and thence to the Freedman's Bureau—all the while maintaining his dependency.

One of the first acts of independence of the Negro was to segregate worship. One of the more popular preachers was "Pappy" George Dupuy. While a slave of a Reverend Craig in Lexington, Dupuy had preached to the Pleasant Green Baptist Church. The death of his master in 1847 brought a crisis to the congregation until William M. Pratt, a white Baptist minister, agreed to purchase Dupuy and allow his congregation to redeem him. This was done just in time for freedom. Dupuy moved to Paducah and founded the Washington Street Baptist Church, where blacks could worship without being subject to white supervision. The church had been organized in 1854 as the African Baptist Church and was served by the white minister of First Baptist until the end of the war.[150]

In politics, Kentucky chose to join the Confederacy in 1866. That year, the conservative wing of the Democratic Party lost control of the state to a faction heavily laced with ex-Confederates. Rather than recognize these returning warriors, many conservatives left the party and joined with the more moderate wing of the opposition to form the modern Republican Party in Kentucky. Radical Republicans lost their influence as the army and the Freedman's Bureau pulled out of Kentucky. In these unsettled times, the role of the Negro was critical, particularly after 1872, when the terms of the Fifteenth Amendment guaranteed that males over twenty-one years of age of all races could vote.

From the end of the Civil War until the Nixon era, the entire Purchase region of Kentucky has voted Democratic. The situation in Paducah differed from that in the rest of the region. The Democrats never were able to exercise complete domination over the Republicans in the political arena; in fact, the Republicans had sufficient support to capture city offices on many occasions. The county vote tipped elections toward the Democrats on more than one occasion during the period before the First World War. The balance of power between the two parties frequently rested with the blacks. This remained true until the city changed its form of government to that of the mayor-commission arrangement to avoid partisan politics in local elections.

The *Daily News* reflected the growing of the reorganized Republican Party in 1875. The paper reported the candidacy of several Democrats for the office of mayor but feared a Republican victory. It was right. A convention of Republicans met in 1884, and about half of those present were black, including the secretary, Sam E. Wharton. The *Daily Republican* and the *Paducah Republican* were published in 1887 and 1888, both edited by L.W. Falls. Even the Democratic papers tried to court the Negro ballot during the late 1800s. The *Daily News* had a regular feature of two columns devoted to "Old Red," who was supposed to be a Negro and advised his race to vote Democratic and suspect the motives of the Republicans.[151]

In 1881, the Southern Democrats captured the city government in Paducah with the election of Charles Reed as mayor. Reed was the first returned Rebel to gain recognition at the polls, and he also was the first native-born Paducahan to serve as mayor. In fact, Reed served from 1881 until 1891, which remains the longest continuous tenure in office. A staunch Democrat, Reed promised a new era; however, the Republicans were not dead.

A part of the appeal and strength of the Republicans lay in their control of federal patronage. The postmaster frequently exercised control over the local party machinery through his control of federal jobs. From 1861 until 1913, the Democrats occupied the White House on only two occasions—the split terms of Grover Cleveland in 1885 and 1893; therefore, membership in the Republican Party offered possibilities of obtaining lucrative positions on the federal payroll.

Reed was followed by Joseph H. Johnson, David A. Yeiser Sr., James M. Lang and Yeiser again in the period from 1889 until 1908. The form of government also changed during this period. The term of office for mayors was extended to four years, and Paducah became a second-class city.

The Republicans recaptured the office of mayor in 1907. The *Daily News-Democrat* was shocked at the returns of November 5. The paper had conducted its own poll during the election and predicted a Democratic victory by 2,306 to 1,865; however, the actual results proved to be a rout of the Democrats. James P. Smith won the mayor's race 2,331 to 2,041. John J. Dorian became the Republican treasurer. The Democrats did put J.W. Orr, Maurice McIntrye and Sam Beadles in as assessor, clerk and jailer. Republicans won the aldermanic seats by four to one and dominated the councilmen by five to two. In addition, all but one of the school board trustees were Republican. In a word, the Republicans controlled Paducah.[152]

During the next four years, the city saw a new political power emerge within the Republican ranks. Thomas Needham Hazelip tried to unseat

Alben Barkley for county judge in 1909 but failed. Hazelip did make a strong showing that encouraged his ambitions for power. From his office at 126½ Fourth Street, Hazelip began building a political base for the next election. Particular attention was given to cultivating black Republicans. Hazelip also sought to overcome or nullify the older party structure that looked to Postmaster Frank Fisher for leadership in party matters. A split in the ranks gave Hazelip his opportunity.

The Republicans met in convocation in July 1911 to pick representatives for the party ticket to be presented to the state convention in Louisville. The local convention endorsed Ed Farley, son of Paducahan Will Farley, then state treasurer. At the state meet, the more progressive element in the party gave its support to Senator A.J. Oliver rather than Farley, and Oliver won the nomination. The Paducah delegation felt that it had been mistreated and blamed the county chairman, E.E. Bell, a young protégé of Fisher. The resulting split in the Republican ranks allowed Hazelip to slip in and gain ascendancy in the party. The partisan *News-Democrat* gloated over the discord in the Republican camp and remarked that Hazelip was "concocting a scheme to kidnap the colored members of the circle and build up a little circle of his own."[153]

Hazelip announced his candidacy for mayor. Earl "the Pearl" Palmer, representing the more conservative Republican interests, also announced. Many still felt that Fisher was in a pivotal position to select the party ticket. At the meeting held on July 25 to determine if the party would have a convention or a primary, Hazelip opted for a primary, while Palmer wanted to continue the traditional convention. Hazelip realized that his forces were in the minority at the meeting, so he agreed on the convention.[154]

While the Republicans quarreled over their mayoral candidate, Paducah swelled by eight to ten thousand during the celebration of August 8, 1911. Negroes came to Paducah from Memphis, Cairo, St. Louis, Louisville and Hopkinsville for the annual observation of the day in 1863 when black soldiers escorted leading Rebel white families to exile in Canada. The park at Rowlandtown and the fairgrounds were reserved for the black festivities—not formally but tacitly. Perhaps the presence of so many black faces was symbolic of their importance in the coming election.[155]

At the Republican convention held on August 18, 1911, Hazelip won the nomination for mayor over Palmer. Others on the ticket included E.M. Willis for treasurer; J.D. Smith for clerk; J.C. Reavis for jailer; John J. Clark for assessor; T.T. Neely for attorney; and George Oelschlaeger Jr., Charles Van Meter, C.C. Duvall and S.L. Tick for aldermen. Walter Matthews, H.T. Vogel, J.P. Ford, August Budde, Frank Mayer and R.S. Barnett stood for councilmen.

"Meet me at the clock." Paducah landmark, Fourth and Broadway.

Hazelip's forces carried the chair of the convention with the help of black voters, who were reported to be in such numbers as to block the street from Fourth to Fifth on Kentucky Avenue. Supporters of the two factions paraded through the hall to cast their ballots for chairman. E.E. Bell, county chairman, lacked sufficient experience to rule in favor of the Fisher forces. Once Arthur Martin, the Hazelip supporter, was in the chair, the issue was decided. Both sides claimed that delegates from the other faction made more than one trip through the hall to vote; however, Chairman Martin declared Hazelip to be the party nominee.[156]

In addition to the Democrats and the Republicans, there was a Socialist ticket in the city election of 1911. The candidates of this party were selected at a meeting that took place on November 7 at a rally held at Fourth and Broadway. The meeting was disrupted by catcalls and boisterous behavior by bystanders; however, the Socialists cut into the Democrat vote at the polls thus allowing the Republicans to emerge victorious.[157]

Victory by the Hazelip faction at the polls in 1911 marked the end of the Democratic Party's domination in Paducah. Hazelip carried the mayor's office by 1,824 to 1,662. The Democrats kept certain city posts. Roscoe Reed was city attorney, Don P. Marton was treasurer, Maurice McIntyre was clerk and James Clark was jailer. The rest of the contested council, aldermanic and school board races went to the Republicans. Hazelip let it be known that heads would roll—Democratic heads.[158]

During his tenure as mayor, Hazelip had to deal with a major flood. In 1913, the city watched with growing agitation the slow progress of high water down the Ohio. By the end of March, Louisville suffered, and the Ohio at Paducah was rising at the rate of two feet per day. A crest was expected in five days. On April 1, Hazelip announced that Paducah would finance and control its own relief efforts. The mayor proudly proclaimed that no outside aid was needed. B.W. Cornelison, an attorney, and William F. Bradshaw Jr., a banker, organized the relief efforts. Earl Palmer chaired the emergency committee. The city waited for a crest of fifty-six feet. Refugees were to go to emergency camps that were set up at Gregory Heights. The city had done all that was possible; now it could only wait.[159]

On April 7, the river crested at 54.3 feet. This was one-tenth higher than the flood of 1884. The paper proudly proclaimed that "Paducahans didn't let this flood bother them any more than the Paducahans of 1884 were bothered by that river rampage."[160]

The election of November 5, 1913, proved to be another turning point for the Republican Party in Paducah. The Democrats took heart at the successful candidacy of Woodrow Wilson for the office of president. Democrats carried other offices as well. The Democrats of Paducah won the race for police judge by six hundred votes, all aldermanic posts by over eight hundred and the county by more than two thousand. The state contest also went to the Democrats. The Republicans faced a grim future—especially since the voters in Paducah reversed their 1911 stand on the commission form of government for Paducah and approved that modification to be effective in 1915. There would be fewer posts all around.[161]

Hazelip sought some device to maintain his political base in Paducah. To this end, he encouraged a secret group called the United Protective Association, organized in 1914 with Hazelip as "chief counselor and advisor." Members of this lodge took an oath to obey the orders of the chief counselor and advisor. Further, each member swore, "I do now seal this oath with my signature in the presence of the officers and members of this post in blood, and swear that only death will separate me from this organization or its secrets, so help me God."[162] Opponents of Hazelip later claimed that the secret organization controlled over 90 percent of the black voters in Paducah, or approximately 1,400 votes.[163]

Not content to rely entirely on black voters to keep him in office, Hazelip became a principal in the Independent Club, which consisted of eight hundred white members.[164] Backed by these two organizations, Hazelip counted on continued control of local politics.

Paducah showed signs of increasing racial pressure by 1916. Denigrating images of blacks were common in the newspaper. Whites enjoyed *Lower Berth*

13, a comedy in blackface at the Kentucky Theater, while *The Birth of a Nation* played at the movies, extolling the virtue of the Ku Klux Klan as the preserver of civilization from the threat of racial mongrelization. Also, the local Elks minstrel show allowed whites to gambol and frolic in their interpretation of black behavior. This attitude persuaded many blacks to join Hazelip's United Protective Association (UPA) as an outlet for "black political aspirations."[165]

Whites viewed the UPA with alarm. The *News-Democrat* reported that a "mob" had attacked the house of Dr. H.T. Haessig at Eighth and Jackson. Dressed in white capes and black caps, the "mob" turned out to be only eight people, including six women. They did march before the house—protesting testimony Haessig's wife had offered in a case involving bootlegging.[166]

In the election of 1915, Ernest Lackey defeated fellow Democrat Frank N. Burns by 248 votes in a hotly contested race for the office of mayor. George C. Wallace, Thomas N. Hazelip and Charles Van Meter kept the Republicans in control of the commission. L.A. Washington was the only Democrat to win a commission seat. F.E. Graves, Wynn Tully, Don P. Marton and W.A. Gardner were defeated. Police had been at every poll to prevent fraud. "Every illegal voter will be challenged and sworn," vowed Luther Graham, chief of police "Offenders will be arrested on the spot."[167]

Many felt that the election had been corrupt. Hazelip received a "night rider" warning on January 29. A note, with skull and crossed bones plus an attached revolver cartridge, was thrown on the doorstep of Commissioner Hazelip during the night or in the early hours of morning. The note alleged that Hazelip gave preference to blacks over whites in employment in the Street Department as payoff for their political support. This charge had merit. Hazelip did support blacks. Such an attitude was not popular in the growing "lily-white" sentiment current in Paducah.[168]

Events in 1916 turned against Hazelip. The Republicans met in late February of that year to select candidates, and a split developed within the party between the Hazelip faction and that supporting Elwood Neel. The following March 1, Hazelip was defeated in his bid to represent the party at its national convention. Not daunted, Hazelip announced his intention to once again oppose Alben Barkley—this time for Congress; however, J.C. Speight of Mayfield beat Hazelip out of the party nomination.[169]

Hazelip's influence was on the wane. On July 5, Judge William Reed of the circuit court at Paducah received a suit against Hazelip and others charging that their election had been fraudulent. Reed granted an injunction on the following day and then quashed it immediately. This maneuver allowed the case to go directly to the court of appeals and be heard by any one judge. Actually, Settle, Carrol and Hurt heard the appeal, and the full court participated in the decision. On July 17, the election of Mayor Lackey and Commissioners Hazelip, Wallace and Van Meter was voided. Only L.A. Washington's election was not challenged. Burns and others claimed that Hazelip controlled over 1,400 of the 1,646 Negro voters in the city through intimidation via threats and secret blood oaths. The charge cited the constitution of the United Protective Association and noted that if anyone attempted to violate his oath, he expected to go "up yonder," meaning to Eddyville State Penitentiary. Hazelip was styled as the "king of the Negroes of Paducah" and charged with playing on the ignorant and superstitious blacks and "putting in fear" the voters.[170]

The appeal was heard by the full court of appeals, chaired by Shackleford Miller; therefore, the decision to nullify the election had the full weight of the commonwealth behind it. Paducah was without a mayor, if only for a time. In a short time, there were three sets of officials contending for control of the government of Paducah. Governor A.O. Stanley, a Democrat, reappointed Ernest Lackey as the mayor, along with Commissioners George Wallace and two newcomers: Hal S. Corbett and Sanders E. Clay.[171] Two days later, the lone commissioner elected by the people of Paducah, L.A. Washington, exercised his office and appointed Zack Bryant as commissioner. Then, the two of them appointed Don P. Marton. Now having three commissioners, E.J. Paxton was appointed and made mayor pro tempore. Not to be outdone, Hazelip claimed he was actually the mayor since the city charter provided that he was to remain in office as mayor until replaced by "a duly elected" successor.[172]

The courts got into the controversy again by mandating a new election to resolve the contending claims. On October 21, 1916, the voters went to the polls to determine which candidates would appear on the November ballot. Three candidates for mayor made the cut. They were Frank Burns, C.L. Van Meter and Ernest Lackey. Five names remained among those contending for seats on the commission: Hazelip, R.R. Treadway, F.E. Graves, Don Marton and John R. Scott. The two appointed by Governor Stanley were dropped (Sanders E. Clay and Hal S. Corbett). Hazelip led the field on the commission side.[173]

For a while, some felt that Burns, Graves and Marton would combine into a Democratic slate; however, the three publically denied this charge.[174] However, there was another incident that did damage the chances of some of the candidates.

On the day prior to the November election, Patrolman H.W. Vick of the "Gash" District claimed that Eulal Smallman was operating a player piano in a bawdy house contrary to the law. This incident was a part of the growing conflict between Judge Cas Crossland and a reform element in the city and the city officials, particularly Mayor Lackey, commissioner of public safety Sanders Clay and chief of police James W. Eaker. The judge claimed that Lackey and Clay permitted houses to operate if they kept pianos quiet and did not burn porch lights. Eaker took out an affidavit denying the charge. Crossland, Vick and Emma Martin swore additional affidavits claiming that Lackey, Clay and Eaker knew of the house. The result was a row that drew comment in the community and might have affected the fortunes of Lackey. There was an unusually heavy turnout for the election.[175]

For a while, it appeared that the national election of 1916 would be a real cliffhanger. The nation was uncertain whether Woodrow Wilson or Charles Evans Hughes had won the presidency. In Paducah, however, there was no doubt about the outcome of the local election. The *Paducah Evening Sun* headed the results with "Hazelip Powers Flicker Out in City Elections—Leader of Clan, Tail-lights on Receding Wagon of Ancient Orders." Burns won the mayoral race by 149 votes. F. Eugene Graves took over public safety; W. Armour Gardner, property; Don P. Marton, finance; and incumbent L.A. Washington became the commissioner of public works. Hazelip was the last man on his own ticket. Lackey went back to his insurance office, while Clay and Corbett resumed their law practices. Heads rolled in the police department. Paducah settled down to worry over the gathering storm in Europe.[176]

The First World War produced a wave of patriotism in Paducah. The nation marshaled men, resources and opinion. Sacrifice was honorable; therefore, the city did not question the economic consequences such as the demise of the Paducah Traction Company. This firm, operated by Stone Webster of Boston, went into receivership early in September 1918, despite the efforts of Stone Webster to revive the firm. Extensive improvements had been made, such as the construction of a brick car barn on West Broadway and the double tracking of Broadway between Fourth and Seventeenth Streets. The number of fares declined as the war progressed, causing the company to petition the city for permission to raise rates from five cents to seven cents per fare. Instead of reducing the deficit, the losses grew, perhaps indicative of an elastic demand for the service. Red ink in the company books reached a point of no return, and the company failed.[177]

Other hardships resulted from the war effort. The *News-Democrat* for September 5, 1918, reported on the first page that "Saloon Revenue Loss

Exceeding $28,000 Imminent" as a result of the passage of the Eighteenth Amendment outlawing liquor. Fifty-three saloons faced forced closing. Even then, the saloonkeepers were asked to make additional sacrifices. As the Spanish influenza epidemic grew, public houses were shut early to avoid spreading the deadly disease. On October 19, saloons were ordered to close at 6:30 p.m. daily.[178]

Individuals rushed to volunteer their services to the armed forces—men who did not face the draft, that is. The community became accustomed to the prospect of the draft via a series of daily releases during the month of September 1918, until the twelfth, when actual registration took place. At the same time, a "role of honor" appeared on the front page listing casualties from the nation at large.[179] "Work or fight" was the charge to young men between eighteen and forty-five years of age. One poignant example of the dedication to the nation involved Conroy Dorian, who had enlisted in the navy. While in training at Great Lakes, Conroy caught influenza and died. Eight days later, his brother, Charles Dorian, replaced Conroy in his nation's service.[180]

Another way Paducahans contributed to the war effort was to observe certain days as special days of abstinence. September 15, 1918, was declared to be "gasolineless" by Charles Wheeler, fuel administrator. The chief of police, Henry Bailey, promised that any driver ignoring the order in the city would be arrested, either by the police or by uniformed "Home Guards."[181]

As the war in Europe ground to a deadly conclusion, the homefront had its most difficult fight. Flu and death went hand in hand in Paducah and elsewhere. On October 23, 73 new cases of flu and 7 new cases of pneumonia were reported. On that date, there were 1,555 cases of flu and 12 cases of pneumonia in the city. Twenty-four deaths occurred. By the end of the month, forty deaths saddened the community. There were 2,008 cases of flu and 166 cases of pneumonia in all. Drastic measures were required. Schools, churches and all public gatherings were cancelled. The measures to control the epidemic ended on the same day that the German Kaiser abdicated. Both events announced that the end was in sight. The years of sacrifice were over.[182]

Paducah emerged from the turmoil of the First World War with a sound economy, and prospects seemed bright. Several new industries had picked Paducah since 1917. In late October 1918, George Goodman, president of the board of trade in Paducah, announced the recent arrival of the Lack Redford Elevator Company. A. Lee Redford of Morganfield, Union County, picked Paducah for his grain operation. Other newcomers were the Muller-Blackledge-Nellis Company, H.P. Hawkins (a corn and flour mill), the Paducah Spoke Company and J.F. Keibler and Company (wholesalers in grain). In addition, the American Cigar Company and the Paducah Hosiery Mill had expanded their operations in the city.[183]

In the fall of 1919, Paducahans were pleased to learn that two former residents still cherished boyhood memories of Paducah and were willing to purchase a plot for a new high school. The only stipulation of Frederick and Sidell Tilghman was that the school should be named for their mother: Augusta Tilghman. The mother and two sons were the family of Confederate general Lloyd Tilghman, the only general from Paducah. They had left the city for Clarksville, Tennessee, on the last boat up the river from Paducah before Kentucky declared for the Union in 1861. In 1870, the younger Tilghman went to New York City and prospered as a broker. Upon learning that Dr. F.B. Dressler, the federal architect for public building, was en route to Paducah, the brothers asked Dressler to pick a suitable site for a new high school for the city. Dressler selected the location of the Ferns, a home owned by Mrs. Elbridge Palmer and her sister, Fannie Gould. The school board accepted the offer of the Tilghmans in a letter made public in the *News-Democrat*.[184]

As the fall of 1919 progressed, the city began to turn its attention toward the coming election. Commissioner Hazelip suggested that the fee of election officers be doubled to four dollars. This was accepted. A large turnout was anticipated. In addition to selecting a slate for the city race, the sewer and school construction bonds were expected to generate interest. Heedless of expected behavior, voters were slow to register. On October 14, the *News-Democrat* urged all voters to qualify for the coming election. High school students canvassed the town in an effort to turn out a large vote favoring the new school bonds for Tilghman High School. Over 2,000 voters had not qualified on the last day prior to the deadline. Efforts of the paper and the students proved successful; over 7,266 voters qualified. This was the heaviest registration in the history of the city. Of the late registration, 1,473 were women. Totals included 2,657 Democrats and 2,283 Republicans. The total number of women enrolled was 2,291. In the election of 1918, 1,625 Democrats and 1,085 Republicans had registered.[185]

Only one candidate was ousted in the primary for the city election. W.A. Gardner lost his bid for a slot on the ballot for November. Two Republicans remained in the race for mayor: F.W. Katterjohn and T.N. Hazelip. Commission candidates included Emmett Bagby, Louis M. Brooks, Milas J. Clark, W.V. Eaton, Jesse Gilbert, Wynn Tully, Mike Williams and James Woolridge.[186] Hazelip ran on what he styled as the "People's Ticket," as he had in 1917; however, this time Hazelip's slate made a clean sweep in the primary. Hazelip led his opponent by 1,962 to 1,950. Tully led the list for commissioner.[187]

Before the election, the bright prospects envisioned by the community at the end of the war began to turn sour. Winter approached. Strikes in the nation's coalfields threatened shortages of fuel for the cold weather ahead.[188] The national mood changed from joy to apprehension.

The election of 1919 was characterized by much "mud slinging." Hard words were exchnged in what the newspaper called a "very close and very warm" campaign.[189] On the final day before the election, Hazelip supporters met in the Kentucky Theater to hear the "People's Ticket" candidates make their final appeal for support. It was not enough. Katterjohn won the mayor's race by 86 votes: 2,370 to 2,284. Eaton, Tully, Gilbert and Williams made the commission. Paducah voters accepted the school bonds in every precinct; the sewer bond issue was rejected. Moreover, the voters reaffirmed the retention of the commission form of government in Paducah. On the state level, the city voted for Edwin P. Morrow, a Republican, for governor, and he was successful.[190]

In the fall of 1922, labor violence associated with the nationwide railroad strike spilled over into Paducah. Homes were fired on. Three bombs exploded in the city on September 1. One was detonated at 229 Harahan at the home of the master mechanic of the Illinois Central Shops, Joseph F. Walker. Another went off at 1900 Trimble at S.E. Stanley's house. Stanley also worked for a railroad as a car repairer. The third bomb damaged the house of Mrs. O.M. Fields at 1326 Langstaff Avenue, perhaps as a warning to Mrs. Fields's brother, also employed by the Illinois Central. Headlines in the local papers blamed the bombings on "reds" and called for action. The following day, Stanley and his neighbor, James Drew, whose house had been fired on earlier, saw two men in the neighborhood acting suspiciously. The men ran, and the two fired six shots at them as they chased the pair through Oak Grove Cemetery. No harm was done.[191]

The United States marshal for western Kentucky, Thomas Needham Hazelip, dispatched two deputies from Louisville to assist local law enforcement efforts to apprehend the bombers. Two men were arrested, but one was released by the federal district court. The other served six days in the county jail for disregarding a court injunction.[192]

While concerned over the labor violence, Paducahans were optimistic that national efforts would resolve the railroad problem. There was a local issue that attracted considerable attention. A petition circulated suggesting that the commission form of government was not needed. Over three thousand signed the instrument, and the matter was put on the ballot in November. The *News-Democrat* tried to sway the election by supporting the existing form; however, the voters, by three to one, elected to return to the alderman-councilman form of government in one of the lightest votes in the history of the city. Only Scott Precinct, containing the residences near Seventh and Broadway, favored retaining the commission form. Partisan politics returned to local election.[193]

In 1923, the city prepared to elect a new administration. The Ku Klux Klan made an effort to gain recognition in Paducah before the election. A national organizer, Dr. E.H. Laugher, announced his plan to speak at the tobacco warehouse at Tenth and Broadway. Dr. J.R. Crawford, pastor of the Kentucky Avenue Presbyterian Church, assailed the hooded knights and denounced the "whole pesky band," who took it upon themselves to be the conscience of "100% Americans." Mayor pro tem L.A. Washington and Commissioner Wynn Tully joined with Claude C. Pace, commissioner of public safety, in opposition to the Klan rally. The city officials sent eighteen police to watch the Klan and prevent any violence. A hostile crowd, numbering between 350 and 500, gathered. Some came out of curiosity; some crossed over the street after leaving the Elks' circus to see what was happening. Finally, the Klansman gave up trying to speak.[194]

Female candidates from both parties ran in the city election. Mrs. Joe F. Post ran for alderman on the Democratic ticket. Mrs. Frances Allen opposed Republican John J. Dorian successfully for treasurer. Mrs. Belle Kinsolving vied with Democrat Ross Rutter for city clerk.[195] Generally, the Democrats were successful, carrying the state and the county elections. Dr. J.N. Bailey, with the backing of Hazelip's Republican organization, not only won the office of mayor but also carried five precincts that were traditionally Democratic. The city of Paducah had Republican mayors for four of the five full terms since 1908. Only during the disputed election of 1916 did the Democrats manage to get control of the office of mayor, and then it took the court of appeals, the governor and a special election.[196]

Democrats carried the city elections in 1924, with the exception of one council seat (Fleming beat Bougeno). Despite this vote, the city gave a plurality to the Republicans in the national contest; however, the county vote put McCracken County into the Democratic camp.[197]

Paducahans learned to regret their hasty decision to return to the mayor-general council form of government. The system was inefficient and cumbersome. Moreover, partisan political issues often clouded local races. Reform was desired. During the 1926 election, the Democrats won all ten vacancies on the general council. Voters also opted to return to the commission form of government, but Kentucky law did not permit cities to change their form of organization during the term of city treasurers, clerks and jailers; therefore, the change could not occur prior to January 1, 1928. There was no doubt about the sentiment of the people. The vote for the commission form was carried by 2,234 to 466.[198]

Elections in 1927 came at a time of prosperity. Alben Barkley had steered a bill through Congress that promised growth for Paducah. A contract for $2 million had been awarded to the Paducah, Ohio River Bridge Company (to build the Irvin S. Cobb Bridge). Work began in the fall. Also, the Illinois Central shops were opened. A special edition of the paper commemorated the dedication of the giant plant. A list of local industries appears to confirm the prosperity of Paducah.[199]

In the contest for mayor, G.W. Dunbar opposed Ernest Lackey and lost, 2,718 to 4,315. Mrs. Bess Maker Howell lost in her bid to be the commissioner of public finance. Ross Rutter earned 3,707 votes to 3,126 for Mrs. Howell. The race for public safety commissioner was not as close. Jack W. Nelson bested Edgar T. Washington by 4,004 to 2,696. Rumsey Bradshaw defeated A.E. Cole for public works commissioner, and George A. Hannin took public property over Will F. Farley by 3,685 to 3,040.[200] Partisan politics did not enter the contest in the city election with the return to the commission form. This situation was most unlike the national races the following year.

As the elections of 1928 neared, Paducah continued to grow prosperous and progressive. The city had recorded large gains for businesses. The local papers, on October 20, 1928, listed new firms on their front pages. Preparations were underway for the bridge over the Ohio. This promised to open the Illinois market to Paducah merchants as never before. The new Cobb Hotel was going up steadily. Prosperity seemed to favor the Republicans. A record vote turned out to determine a new president. Only four of the thirty-four precincts in Paducah voted for Al Smith. Herbert Hoover and the Republican Party carried both the city and the state; however, the First District remained Democratic.[201]

The Depression disrupted Paducah, like other cities across the nation, and turned Paducahans toward the Democratic camp. One main factor in this transformation here and elsewhere was the realignment of the black vote. The party of Lincoln lost the unquestioning loyalty of black Americans. The primary election of 1931 attracted considerable interest, and this continued over into the general election. Ed Scott defeated B.A. Washburn for mayor.

Other winners included Charles C. Rieke for finance over Ross Rutter and Emmet Holt for safety over Wells Heath. George Block took property over George Hannin, while E.R. Bradshaw defeated E.L. Ross for public works. The "outs" continued to replace the "ins."[202]

Paducah changed administrations twice between the crash of the great bull stock market and the awful destruction of the flood of 1937. While not spectacular, these administrations had to deal with the growing problems of unemployment and insecurity that accompanied the Depression. It was during these years that a group of civic-minded Paducahans undertook a remarkable assignment: to create a college for the youth of the city. At a time when one out of every four workers in the nation was on unemployment, Paducah started a junior college. The creation of Paducah Junior College was an act of faith that defied the despair prevalent in many communities in 1932.

Washburn was successful in the 1935 election for mayor, narrowly defeating Jack Nelson. In fact, Nelson led for a time, as he had in the October primary. Along with B.A. Washburn, Herbert S. Melton, George A. Hannin, Tuttle Lockwood and Dr. S.B. Pulliam won seats on the city commission.[203]

Like most communities in the nation, Paducah suffered from the Depression, but it was more fortunate than most. The state director of the Works Project Administration (WPA) was George Goodman of Paducah. Mr. Goodman was a close personal friend of Senator Alben Barkley; thus, he had a direct link to President Roosevelt. Kentucky was organized into six districts under the WPA, Paducah being in District One, which ranged from Owensboro to Madisonville. Branch offices were in Paducah, Mayfield and Clinton. John F. Costello was in charge of the office in Paducah with Earl Steinhauer assisting as assignment officer.[204]

The Goodman Papers at the Margaret I. King Library of the University of Kentucky–Lexington include semimonthly reports of all WPA projects in the state with pictures illustrating progress. A sample of such projects illustrates the wide range of interests served. Schools were painted.[205] Additional schools were built.[206] The city of Paducah got a playground, a new water line and improvements in the courthouse, to name but a few.[207] Deeds were cross-indexed.[208] A stadium and athletic field for the Augusta Tilghman High School was completed. The 400,000 bricks for the project were made on-site by an old black man and a mule.[209] A swimming pool, one hundred by two hundred feet, gave the city the largest recreational swimming pool west of Louisville.[210]

Riverside Park (now Barkley Park) was completed.[211] The location of WPA workers in Paducah proved to be most helpful, especially during the devastating flood of 1937.

Chapter 6

FLOODS

Paducah suffered from several natural disasters, but none equaled the devastation of the flood of 1937. The first week in February 1902 is remembered as the "White Week." The city was coated in ice. Trees, wires, roofs—nearly everything exposed to the elements felt the heavy blow of the storm. The damage was estimated at $200,000.[212] In 1913, floodwaters surpassed the high-water mark of 1884, but no major damage resulted. That was not the case in the winter storm of 1917. Sixteen inches of snow fell on December 8. More snow followed to a depth of twenty-four inches by January 13, 1917. The following night, the Ohio froze to a depth of eight inches; people walked on the river without fear. When the ice broke just before dawn on January 29, a great roar announced that the pack was moving, carrying with it boats and barges. Two days later, the ice on the Tennessee surged through the "chute" formed by Owen Island, scouring the Paducah riverfront. Damage to river craft reached $1 million; still, compared to 1937, these events were only a minor hindrance to the progress of the city.[213]

In 1937, floodwaters topped the previous mark by 6.5 feet. Worse, each flood seemed to be getting progressively more destructive. The flood of 1867 reached 50.7 feet. In 1884, the high-water mark was 54.2 feet, a record that was surpassed by one-tenth in 1913. The public image of Paducah changed from viewing the site as relatively high ground to suspicion that the location was potentially dangerous for business and residential structures. For a time, the growth of the city hung in the balance. The construction of a floodwall

The flood of 1937, which forced twenty-four thousand people to leave Paducah.

in the 1940s changed the stalemate and enabled the community to regain its appeal to new business.[214]

January 1937 opened with rain that continued through the first two weeks, but Paducahans did not worry. Bobby Marshall, wife of Dr. T.J. Marshall, kept a record of her experiences during the flood. She recalled that "occasionally we would hear someone say that the river was very high, but as Paducah had always been high and dry when other cities and towns on the Ohio and Tennessee were flooded, we felt no uneasiness."[215] Instead, citizens of Paducah basked in the success of the city during the previous year. City manager L.V. Bean remarked on January 3, "I think we have just closed a most satisfactory year."[216] Not until January 10 did people begin to take notice of the rising water.

An ice and sleet storm paralyzed Paducah on January 10. "We had the worst sleet storm Paducah has ever experienced," wrote Mrs. Marshall. All the beautiful shade trees were ruined, "all the telephone, telegraph, and electric light wires were completely wrecked."[217] Kentucky Utilities repairmen were working day and night to recover electricity for the community. People who had stokers and "who cooked with electricity had to close their homes and go to the hotels or to the homes of friends or relatives in order to keep warm or have food."[218] Wires were repaired after several days, and everyone felt the worst was over. Actually, the flood was just beginning.[219]

The flood came with surprising speed. Utter isolation compounded the problems generated by the high water. Telephone, telegraph and even the local radio station went silent. People could only watch the water rise and hope that friends and neighbors were safe. On Thursday, January 21, people in the downtown area began talking about the backwater that was creeping into the lower areas of the city. As Mrs. Marshall wrote, "Nobody felt that Paducah was in any danger. Certainly we never dreamed that our part of town would be inundated." Dr. Marshall went on a call, and by the time he headed for home, water was about two feet deep at Nineteenth and Broadway, two blocks from the Marshall house at 110 Fountain Avenue. The following day brought more sleet and rapidly rising backwater that quickly covered Kentucky, Broadway, Jefferson and Monroe Streets at Tenth through Thirteenth Streets. Temperature readings indicated a rapid drop, which caused automobile engines to freeze, and before many of these stalled cars could be recovered, the waters closed over them. They remained as a hazard to navigation when boats replaced automobiles on the streets. Waves from passing boats also bounced the hulks about, making their destruction total.

At first, employers downtown insisted that their workers stay at the Cobb Hotel. After a while, electricity failed. One blanket per person did not protect the guests from the cold. All had to be evacuated to refugee camps on the higher ground in the west end.

Downtown during 1937 flood. *Courtesy of Mayor Tom Wilson.*

The city finally realized that some extraordinary measures were needed. On January 19, Charles G. Vahlkamp, chairman of the Red Cross, appointed emergency committees. The following day, refugees were housed in the old Southern Hotel at Second and Broadway. Water had closed Jefferson at First Street. The gauge was at fifty-one feet, and officials warned that another rise would mean disruption of electric service. The loss of power isolated Paducah. "The thing that made the situation so distressing in Paducah," recalled Mrs. Marshall, "was that right from the start every means of communication was completely wrecked by that sleet storm, even WPAD radio station, and for three days and nights, the outside world knew nothing of our desperate plight."[220]

A medical center was established at Clark School. Dr. Marshall ministered to stranded Paducahans as best he could. "He would row up to a pretty brick house [the smaller one-story homes were evacuated first, as they were soon submerged], open the front door, row in the front hall or living room, tie the boat to the banister, step over the banister to the second floor and minister to the patient and so on to the next and the next." After several days, "the Red Cross got things pretty well organized, and after consulting with the local doctors, health department and city officials, they decided that the entire city must be evacuated—there were too many hazards. No sanitation whatsoever, no water ['water, water all around and not a drop to drink']." Riverside Hospital was evacuated first and then the hotels. The Illinois Central Hospital was the last to be moved. The dead were moved to second floors of the different funeral homes until they could be evacuated.

Ethel Pell Hannin of 2503 Park Avenue took refuge on the second floor of her home. There, she wrote to her sister Dorris Settle, who lived in Michigan. On January 23, Ethel wrote, "We are waterbound. Will have to move upstairs by night fall." She noted that the temperature was down to eighteen degrees. "We are all grouped around the fireplace as this is the only fire we can have. All work is suspended. The Ritz Hotel is inundated."[221]

The following day, January 24, Mrs. Hannin reported dining on sardines and crackers for breakfast: "We are looking out on dozens of cars and trucks nearly submerged in water. All we can see is a small portion of the tops."[222]

The *Paducah Sun-Democrat* for January 30, 1937, was published at Mayfield. Complete evacuation of Paducah was underway. Regular army men under the command of Captain Glen Peterson were to coordinate the move. In a ten-day period, twenty-two thousand people registered as refugees at Arcadia School, a clearing station in the west end. "They went everywhere. Mayfield was jammed. So were the other Paducah neighbors.

Even country schools and churches became the temporary homes of thousands."[223] Even hospitality has a limit. Mary Margaret Hoffman was one of the last to leave Paducah with her father and brothers. They went to Mayfield, where a sign read, "Refugees, Don't Stop Here." Wickliffe was able to accommodate them.[224]

The flood challenged traditional social values as the emergency worsened. In one instance, two young, single refugees found themselves sharing the same bed. Each worked different hours, so they never met; however, the young lady found it embarrassing to admit that she shared a common bed with a young man.[225]

At Lone Oak, refugees were housed in the high school, and the Boy Scouts helped make arrangements for the displaced persons. A local meatpacker agreed to donate meat to help feed the refugees, but snowy roads made it impossible for vehicles to get to the Ross plant on Wildcat Road; therefore, the Scouts, fourteen and fifteen years of age for the most part, walked from the high school to the packinghouse, and each carried about fifty pounds of meat back to the school—approximately six miles round-trip.[226]

Sanitation problems developed at the camp at Lone Oak and elsewhere. The Scouts divided the refugees into family groups where possible, assigning rooms to larger families; others were separated by curtains of blankets. As a result of the crowded conditions, particularly in the restrooms, some families allowed children to use paper sacks and hid the feces behind the old steam radiators. Before long, everyone knew they had a problem, and steps were taken to correct the situation.[227]

The threat of an epidemic caused health officials to insist on mass inoculation against typhoid. Sore arms resulted, but no major outbreak occurred despite the overcrowded conditions in many of the camps.

On February 2, the crest reached 60.8 feet. On the same date, twelve men were arrested for looting. The city jail had been under water for several days, so the offenders were taken to the rear of the Keiler house and held in temporary police headquarters until they could be transported to Mayfield. The following day, another agent of destruction hit Paducah. The closing of the city water plant meant that there was no pressure on the mains, making efforts to cope with fire next to impossible. A fire started in a grain elevator on the south side of Madison between Tenth and Eleventh Streets and spread to nearby houses. Fireman watched helplessly as the structures burned to the water line. A night patrol helped prevent further looting; army patrols and passes limited the number of people with access to the flooded area. The city waited for the waters to ebb so that the slow and painful process of recovery could begin.[228]

Paducah Carnegie Library before the fire. *Dafford Murals.*

Not all was gloom and doom during February. The children from the Friendly Home, along with Miss Vonie Young and Mrs. Phoebe McGee, were having a grand time. These refugees were housed in the Country Club and had a golf course for a recreational area.[229]

The west end took on a new role in the community. No longer devoted to residential housing, the "city" of Avondale housed the offices of the Southern Bell Telephone Company, the U.S. Post Office, the WPA offices and space for the mayor, city government and the jail. Hastily built pine structures were christened "AF" architecture for "after the flood."[230]

Coordination of relief efforts proved to be difficult. Captain Glen Peterson of the Civilian Conservation Corps in Paducah assumed command of all army personnel in the area. The arrival of 150 regular army troops from Fort Sheridan, Illinois, gave Peterson a disciplined force to patrol the flooded city to prevent looting. The troops supervised the complete evacuation of the flooded area by January 30. City manager L.V. Bean announced that he had assumed command of the entire operation on February 1. Ten days later, the board of commissioners decided that Edgar T. Washburn would be in joint control with Bean; however, Bean refused to yield power to the mayor. Police chief William Bryant reported that Bean had told him "to act only on his orders." Despite this disunity, relief efforts continued to function.[231]

Even before the floodwaters dropped below the fifty-six-foot mark, a committee looked to the rebuilding of Paducah. Manager Bean, Con

Number 533 Madison in 1980, home of Alben Barkley Junior Historians.

W. Craig, Harry Meyer, Max Miller and George Runge set goals for repopulating the community. Harry Hopkins of the WPA, Governor A.B. "Happy" Chandler of Kentucky and officials of the state and federal government came to see the extent of the damage and went away impressed at the degree of the devastation. They joined with Senator Alben Barkley of Paducah in urging Congress to pass a federal program to provide low-cost loans to assist in rebuilding the ravaged communities along the Ohio River. On February 13, Tom Waller, a local attorney, went to Washington to represent Paducah at a conference of mayors with Hopkins. Waller urged the consolidation of relief efforts through one agency to ease the red tape. Eventually, fifty-one different agencies pooled their efforts on behalf of flood-stricken cities.[232]

The worst was over when the Red Cross announced the closing of its canteen on February 12. Pete Fowler had been in charge of this operation from the beginning when he broke a window on the Peacock Garden building with the butt of his pistol and opened an emergency food center. Before it closed, the canteen served forty-one thousand meals and employed over 150 workers. The cafeteria at Arcadia replaced the canteen.[233]

"River's Long Reign at End" was the paper's long-awaited announcement on February 18. The stage at 6:00 p.m. the previous evening had been 47.9 feet. Over seven-eighths of the city had been under water for a month, and 22,000 refugees from Paducah had been taken to centers in Kentucky and Tennessee. Now these displaced persons had to return and rebuild.[234] Silt, slime and muck greeted them and had to be removed. All basic services—lights, water, gas, sanitary sewers—had to be renovated. Buildings had to be inspected to see if any structural damage had been sustained before people could return. An inspection committee, including members of the fire department and representatives of local architects, arranged to issue permits to return for residents and businessmen. In the meantime, arrangements were made to house the returning refugees in Paducah schools. Gus G. Meyers, Red Cross chairman, announced that six campsites would be required to meet the additional housing demands until the homeless could return to their own residences. At the time, the Red Cross provided for 5,035 unsettled residents in Paducah.[235] Approximately 4,500 additional spaces were anticipated.[236]

The receding floodwaters exposed more than silt. On February 14, the body of Uel Park, twenty-three, of 1315 Langstaff Avenue was recovered. He had fallen out of a boat and drowned. Park's father survived the mishap by clinging to a pole until rescuers could reach him. Two days later, more bodies were discovered. William and Stella Alcock, both over sixty-five, were found in their three-room house on Pool Road lying in the kitchen. Tom Wall of 1317 Monroe was found in bed wrapped in blankets and was believed to have died before the flood. Jim Beach of 621 Park Avenue also was found in bed, apparently the victim of a heart attack. James Stokes, sixty-one, of 635 Flournoy was discovered wrapped in blankets. None but Park's death was directly related to drowning, but cold, effort and worry took their toll on the ill and the aged. The final victims were not discovered until March 24, when the bodies of Mrs. Emma Skillian and her older sister, Lizzie Petter, were found on the bed of their "gun-barrel" home at 1015 Washington Street. The waters had reached within eighteen inches of the ceiling of the house, and the sisters drowned. The intense cold had delayed discovery of the bodies for more than two months.[237]

One of the first concerns of Paducahans was to avoid the reoccurrence of floods such as that of 1937. On February 19, a town meeting was held to discuss the possible construction of a "seawall" around the city.[238] Two days later, a mass meeting was held to air the topic, and a petition was sent to Congress on February 22.[239] Estimated cost of the levee was $5,300,000, and the project was endorsed by the Rotary Club and the Workers Alliance.[240]

The newspapers of March 7 carried a special section on the flood. Pictures revealed the extent of the damage throughout the Ohio Valley. Edwin B. Greenwald wrote about the Paducah experience that now was history. The sense of isolation was over. Paducahans, some for the first time, realized that, pervasive as the devastation had been, they could empathize with residents of Louisville and Memphis.

The flood caused many changed attitudes in Paducah. Never again did the city feel secure in its elevated position. Only when the floodwall was completed did the apprehension ease. Another result of the flood was the changed status of the piano. WPA workers found more than 2,500 of the estimated 3,200 pianos of the city during the cleanup. The ruined cabinets were taken to the east side of the Illinois Central roundhouse and dumped into a hollow. Entertainment had centered on the piano before the flood in many homes; afterward, the radio gained a greater following. The change meant that Paducahans became consumers of entertainment rather than participants in it.[241]

Chapter 7

POLITICS, 1939–1980

In 1939, predictions were for a heavy turnout of voters. The Associated Press had noted this trend and announced, "More Than Usual Interest Is Displayed in Off-Year Voting." There was no question about the victory in the race for the mayor's office. Pierce Lackey easily defeated Gus Hank Jr. Commissioners were Dr. S.B. Pulliam, George C. Baker and Miss Mary M. Dorian (co-owner of a private school).[242]

The community was more concerned with the prosecution of the war than with local elections in 1943. In fact, the primary "slipped up" on many; a light vote was recorded. The two candidates for mayor were Wayne Seaton and Mary Dorian. The candidacy of the latter was unique at that time in Kentucky for cities of the second class; consequently, the public was not yet ready to admit women to the highest post in the city. Seaton polled 3,497 votes to 2, 710 for Miss Dorian. Commissioners were Dr. S.B. Pulliam again, Stuart Johnston, Harold Wagner and Rudy Pierce (who replaced Miss Dorian on the board).[243]

In 1947, Gene Peak collected 4,145 votes to 3,072 for Rex Cornelison in the contest for mayor. Paul Abel, George A. Allen, Stuart Johnston and Edward Carlick were elected to the board of commissioners. Peak died after being in office for a short time and was replaced by Stuart Johnston, mayor pro tem, until the latter could be confirmed by a special election.[244]

In 1951, the modern age came to Paducah. The *Sun-Democrat* announced it planned to seek a permit to build a television station in Paducah. Tentative zoning plans were discussed on November 4. A bond issue to build three white and two colored schools also attracted attention in a community still segregated. On November 6, it rained, and Paducahans poured the votes into boxes marked Cherry. Young (thirty-six), self-made and a recently returned veteran, Robert Cherry swept the mayor's race, polling 4,029 votes to 911 for J.P. Wilson. Taking office with Cherry were George Jacobs, Robert L. Morrow, Troy Clark and Stuart Johnston. These officials had to deal with the second invasion of the city by hordes of outsiders. The Atomic Energy Commission decision to locate a plant in the city, producing a boom and attendant problems that occupied Paducah during the early 1950s.[245]

The mayoral race in 1955 was unique. George Jacobs won without opposition. Taking office with Jacobs were Ed Trevethan, Morris McBride, H.L. Gangnath and Troy Clark.[246]

If 1955 had been unusual for the lack of opposition in the mayoral race, 1959 was at the other pole. Claims and counter claims between Cherry and the Paxton newspaper livened the contest. As a result, the voter turnout was heavy. The contestants were both young, had been active in civic clubs and were friends. Richard Fairhurst had been instrumental in founding the JCs and, like Cherry, was successful and energetic. Nevertheless, the contest essentially was the rest of Paducah versus the west end, represented by Fairhurst. Cherry won in a controversial contest by 4,238 to 4,222 for Fairhurst. The latter demanded a recount in one black precinct; Cherry and George Jacobs objected. The man in charge of the voting machine refused to allow a recount on the night of the election and stood fast on his decision until threatened with a court order the following day. James L. Munal, a Republican, finally agreed to a recount after the voting machines had been transferred to the courthouse. In the recount, Cherry's lead increased by a few votes. Cherry's margin went from 16 votes to 20 votes.[247]

In 1963, Tom Wilson beat Winston Gholson by 4,510 to 3,957 in the race for the mayor's office. Jimmie Davis, A.B. Findley, W.L. Kressenburg and John Hornsby were elected as commissioners.[248] Wilson had gotten into local politics in an effort to prevent the removal of city hall from the downtown area, which eventually led to the construction of the present building designed by Edward Durell Stone. Unlike other cities, Paducah managed to preserve its central business district.

A precedent was set during the 1967 election in Paducah. No mayor had ever served three four-year terms. David Yeiser had served thirteen years as mayor, but five elections were involved. The election of Robert Cherry, therefore, was a first, and he beat Robert Johnston by 4,993 to 4,410. Among

Right: Bust of Governor Julian Carroll by Fredda Brilliant, lobby, city hall.

Below: First city hall, 1913.

Current city hall, 1980.

the commissioners were Bill Fellers, Tommy Lambert, Henry Puryear and Dolly McNutt, in her first effort in politics.[249]

In 1971, Mrs. Houston McNutt became the first woman to serve as mayor of Paducah by winning over George Bell by 4,889 to 3,538, a margin of 1,351. Dolly carried twenty-two of twenty-eight precincts and tied for another. There was another new element in this election. Clifford Robinson, a black man, ran for mayor in the primary. W.G. Harvey won a commission seat, having served as mayor pro tem after winning reelection in 1969. (Unlike other blacks, Harvey ran his campaign on a broad-based platform that sought support from the entire community, not just the black element.) Others winning seats on the commission in 1971 were Henry Puryear, mayor pro tem; John Hornsby; and Tommy Lambert.[250]

Cherry tried twice more for a fourth term. The first was in 1975, when he was defeated by William Murphy by 4,319 to 3,269. An issue in this campaign was how much time a busy man like Cherry could devote to city affairs. Murphy campaigned on a pledge to be the first "full-time" mayor. Commissioners were Clifford Brumley, P.J. Grumley, Henry Puryear and John Hornsby.[251]

City hall, interior, 1980.

In 1979, Cherry tried again but was defeated by John Penrod, a retired agent of the Federal Bureau of Investigation who was teaching law enforcement at Paducah Community College. Only one commissioner retained his seat, and that was Robert Coleman. Newcomers included James Flynn, Joe Vitersi and Harold "Shorty" Ford.[252]

Chapter 8

INDUSTRY

Paducah originally depended on merchandising and transportation. As the town grew, it became the center of marketing for agricultural products, particularly dark-fired tobacco. The first industry was related to river transportation, and the local marine ways have remained a viable contributor to the prosperity of the community. Railroads came in the decade before the Civil War, and this industry expanded after the war to become the principal employer in the city and the fourth-largest industry in the state. Manufacturing began with lumber products. Light industries, such as hosiery mills, came to Paducah in the early years of this century. The advent of heavy industry followed the Second World War and located outside the corporate limits of the city. In particular, the construction of the atomic plant produced a major transformation in Paducah.

The first industry in Paducah began with the contract between Elijah Lovejoy of St. Louis and the town. Lovejoy was to receive $1,000 for use of his patented marine rail system and another $500 to supervise the construction of the ways. The agreement was reached on August 25, 1843; however, actual operation did not begin until 1854, when eight rail sections capable of holding boats 350 feet in length were completed.[253] Steamboats and barges were built on these ways.

River transportation played a vital role in the development of Paducah. Passing steamboats could buy wood stacked at the Paducah landing for 12½ cents per cord in 1833.[254] By 1842, the riverfront was graded and graveled at a cost of $1,000. This made the arrival of the Fowler wharf boat a welcomed asset to the town. Now, steamboats could fuel and take on needed supplies at one stop. After the Civil War, Gus, Dick, Joe and Joe's wife, Laura, combined with G.C. Grumbaugh to create the Fowler Brothers' and Company. This organization ran packets on four rivers—the Ohio, Mississippi, Cumberland and Tennessee—after the Fowler Brothers combined with the Evansville, Cairo and Memphis Steam Packet Company in March 1881 and reorganized in 1891. The *Dick Fowler*, a packet of the company, made the one-way trip from Cairo to Evansville in fourteen hours and forty-seven seconds—a record. Until 1887, the Evansville and Tennessee River Packet Company ran twice a week from Paducah to Waterloo, Alabama. The transfer of the mail franchise from the river packets to the railroads marked the passing of an era.[255]

The aftermath of the 1937 flood proved to be beneficial to river transport. The call for flood control brought forth both flood and navigational control. Dams on the Ohio kept the water level suitable for use even in the summer. River traffic to Paducah revived in importance. In 2014, Crounse Corporation, Louis Igert, M-G Transport Services, Molloy Marine Service, R&W Marine, Southern Barge Lines, Tolen Marine and Walker Towing Corporation call Paducah home.[256]

Lumbering became a mainstay of Paducah with the establishment of the area known as "Jersey" by James Langstaff. Forty-five acres were purchased in 1847 for $1,200, and a sawmill was set up. Times were favorable to the new enterprise. Over one hundred new houses were erected in Paducah between 1848 and 1849.[257] Jersey began on Island Creek and extended north along present George Street to Sixth and thence west to the creek. The settlement received its name from the fact that Langstaff came from New Jersey. The area prospered. In May 1849, the firm began the manufacture of the 800,000 bricks that were needed for the government marine hospital in Paducah. Approximately 150 men were employed by the firm at this time.[258]

The Langstaff-Orm Company suffered a major disaster in 1905, when a fire destroyed the sawmill department. Damage was estimated at $20,000 to the equipment, which was steam-driven. The mill had been in constant operation for three weeks at the time of the fire. The mill had a capacity of 75,000 to 100,000 feet of lumber per day, and the firm employed 350, about half of whom were assigned to the mill. The firm rebuilt after the fire, but this was not the case after the flood of 1937, which severely damaged the building and equipment of the concern, not to mention the loss of material that floated away. The firm closed in 1939.[259]

The location of a large lumber mill in Paducah helped other firms choose the town for the location of other wood-related products. The Paducah

Furniture Manufacturing Company incorporated in 1870 with a stock of $35,000. Elbridge Palmer served as the president, and Charles H. Reike Jr. was manager. The firm employed about one hundred men and kept four salesmen in the field at one time.[260]

John W. Little gave his name to a part of Paducah when he decided to move his spoke factory from Dresden, Tennessee, late in 1894. The Tennessee site had only one railroad, and Little felt his company was at the mercy of whatever rate the carrier wanted to impose. At the Paducah location, both the Paducah, Tennessee and Alabama and the Chesapeake Ohio and Southwestern lines would have to compete in price; thus, Little could reduce his shipping costs. Little employed between 100 and 150 men. Fire destroyed the main building of the company in 1907. City firemen had difficulty in fighting the fire; the building was just in the city limits, and the firemen had to run hoses five hundred feet to reach the nearest hydrant.[261]

Mechanicsburg had sawmills, furniture factories and other plants based on wood. This section of Paducah adjoins Jersey and runs from the river to the Benton Road. The McKinnie Veneer and Lumber Company ran a large operation in this section of town around 1900. On April 28, 1897, a raft containing 335,000 feet of prime timber out of Tennessee landed at the mouth of Clark's River. Most of the logs were oak and poplar, and one log measured twelve feet long and eight feet, two inches thick. The McKinnie Veneer and Lumber Company burned down on September 27, 1906. Another effort was made to revive the firm at a location at Third and Elizabeth Streets, but that burned, too, on June 25, 1907.[262]

Another major employer in the Mechanicsburg community was the Mergenthaler-Harton Basket Company. The firm opened in 1902, suffered fire damage and eventually went bankrupt. At one time, three hundred people worked for this concern. The principal wood used in the manufacture of baskets was gum. This company had 115 machines designed by Mr. Mergenthaler and Emment Horton. Each machine could produce 2,500 baskets for $4.50 less than if they had been made by hand.[263]

Also in the Mechanicsburg section, the Hollingshead Barrel Factory opened in 1901. Estimated capacity was two thousand barrels per day if a full complement of two hundred workers was used. The firm supplied barrels to the Gregory Vinegar Works of Paducah (about twenty thousand a year). The barrel firm decided to come to Paducah at the urging of the Commerce Club, a local organization that preceded the chamber of commerce as an active agent for searching out additional industries for the city.[264]

The economic downturn of 1907 caused many of the industries in Paducah to fail, particularly those located in Mechanicsburg. A pool of unemployed workers attracted a new type of enterprise to the community. The firms opening plants in the city of Paducah between 1907 and 1940 were marginal—that is, high-cost and low-profit enterprises such as hosiery mills. The success of these firms depended on low wages. As a result, when the operators of these firms gained positions of importance in civic groups such as the Commerce Club, entry of higher-paying firms was discouraged. This attitude helped keep Paducah from growing. Without growth, the city settled into a narrow, self-centered shell. This complacency ended with the advent of the atomic plant.[265]

Chapter 9

STEAM TO THE ATOM

The New Orleans and Ohio Railroad suffered from raids by Forrest and irregulars during the Civil War; however, the Union command kept the railroad repaired since it was a vital link in its communications lines. At the end of the war, the railroad faced financial difficulties. Judge Flournoy succeeded Judge James Campbell as president of the line in 1865. Flournoy was replaced by Lawrence S. Trimble the following year. Despite the efforts of these able men, the company continued to suffer financial decline until February 1869, when the railroad was auctioned off to the highest bidder, Eckstein Norton. The bankrupt line was reorganized as the Paducah and Gulf Railroad Company on February 26, 1869. Two other lines were added on January 31, 1872, with Norton as president. Nevertheless, the company could not survive the panic of 1873. In March 1878, a new organization known as the Memphis, Paducah and Northern emerged to take over the route. In 1881, Collis P. Huntington purchased both the Paducah and Memphis and the Paducah and Elizabethtown railroads and formed them into the Chesapeake, Ohio and Southwestern system with a direct connection between Louisville and Memphis via Paducah.[266]

The Paducah and Elizabethtown Railroad had been authorized by the Kentucky legislature by an act passed on March 5, 1867. Construction began in 1869, and the railroad was opened on September 6, 1872. For the first time, the Purchase region of Kentucky had a direct, all-weather connection with the rest of the state.[267]

After the Paducah and Elizabethtown consolidated with the successor of the New Orleans and Ohio as the Chesapeake, Ohio and Southwestern (CO&SW), the shops of the line were moved from Elizabethtown to Paducah, perhaps at the urging of Q.Q. Quigley, a lawyer famed for his ability as a raconteur, perhaps because Paducah was now the center of the new system. The shops were completed in 1884, making Paducah the principal repair and supply center of the CO&SW. The original shops consisted of a roundhouse of six stalls, a machine shop and a car shop, together with a blacksmith's shop, a boiler shop and a brass foundry. The initial investment in these units was estimated at $107,000.[268]

The financial panic of 1893 forced Huntington to sell part of his holdings, including the CO&SW. The Illinois Central acquired ownership of the system in December 1893; however, a series of lawsuits prevented the transfer of the title until August 1, 1896. Currently, this section is known as the Kentucky Division of the Illinois Central Gulf.[269]

The other major trunk-line railroad entering Paducah was built with the active support of the city. In the council minutes for January 28, 1889, is a record of the agreement of the city to purchase $100,000 of bonds to aid in the construction of the Paducah, Tennessee and Alabama Railroad. Work began immediately. Eventually, this line became part of the Nashville, Chattanooga and St. Louis Railway and, since the Second World War, part of the Louisville and Nashville system. The line runs from Paducah to Bruceton, Tennessee, via Benton, Murray and Paris.[270]

Immediately following the Civil War, Lawrence S. Trimble of Paducah organized the Paducah and Illinois Bridge Company to span the Ohio River. Among the members of the company were John A. Logan and Ambrose E. Burnside, formerly generals in the Federal armies, and P.G.T. Beauregard and Absolom M. West, both generals in the Confederate service. Failure of the project cost Paducah the principal north–south trunk line between Chicago and New Orleans, as the Illinois Central built such a bridge near Cairo on October 29, 1889. Nonetheless, Paducah remained an important railroad town.[271] Eventually, a bridge was built over the Ohio near Paducah.

Paducah spanned the Ohio with the completion of the Paducah and Illinois (P&I) Railroad. This company was chartered in Kentucky but actually involved the Chicago, Burlington and Quincy and the Nashville, Chattanooga and St. Louis Railroads. The firm completed a bridge over the Ohio at Metropolis, Illinois, during the First World War. The great ice storm that year destroyed the transfer ferry of the Illinois Central (ICG, also Illinois Central Gulf) that made daily runs to Brookport from the riverfront

Illinois Central Railroad Shops and Round House, circa 1940. *Courtesy of the William Clark Museum.*

at Paducah; therefore, the ICG began using the P&I bridge on an emergency basis. The arrangement was so useful that it continued. Later, in 1925, the Illinois Central built the 169-mile Edgewood Cutoff to take advantage of the crossing at Metropolis. Currently, the ICG, the Louisville and Nashville (L&N) and the Burlington Northern jointly use the P&I. The location of the TVA Shawnee Steam plant on this short line gave it additional importance in the 1950s.[272]

In 1927, the ICG constructed one of the largest railroad shops in the world at Paducah. This immense plant, covering 110 acres, initially cost $11 million and ranked as the fourth-largest employer in all of Kentucky. Steam locomotives of the 4-8-2 Mountain class were built at this installation; twenty were completed in 1942–43 at a period when the plant was operating at capacity. Still, the workers maintained a remarkable safety record. The shop personnel put in 2,456,776 accident-free man-hours.[273]

Following the Second World War, the shops served as a repair and maintenance point for the ICG and others. With the gradual change from steam to diesel, the shops were converted to service the new engines. The last steam engine refurbished at Paducah was the 2741 between 1957 and 1958. For a time, the shops became the graveyard of steamers. Hundreds of massive steam engines that once pulled up to ninety-nine loads of coal from

The ICG's Mikkado 2-8-2 in Barkley Park in 1980, now at the floodwall at Kentucky and Water Streets.

Dawson Springs south to Paducah went under the cutting torch. Sleek trains became scrap. Even the 2750, the giant of the freight service, was cut up. One Mikkado was preserved and presented to the city as a memorial to the passage of the age of steam.[274]

Since 1968, the shops at Paducah have concentrated on remanufacturing diesel-electric engines. At present, the Paducah operation is international in scope and is the largest of its kind.[275]

During the early days of the Second World War, the Kentucky Ordnance Plant was built near Paducah. The Kentucky Dam on the Tennessee River was completed in 1944. These two events helped trigger a series of decisions that led to the location of the Atomic Energy Commission's (AEC) enriched uranium plant in Paducah. Within a short time, the population of the city doubled. Paducah was hard pressed to accommodate the influx. Business boomed; bank clearings in Paducah showed the greatest increase of any in the nation. Paducah became a national news item. Changes induced during the period still determine the character of the community.

"Billion Dollar Atomic Plant for Paducah!" Paducahans saw that headline in their paper on December 14, 1950.[276] The Cold War made the possession of greater and more powerful atomic weapons a priority. Further, in Asia, North Korean troops invaded South Korea with the open support of Russia. American troops were committed to the battle and managed to throw the invaders back north of the thirty-eighth parallel. Late in the year, the combined United Nations forces were in sight of the Yalu River, which

Robert Dafford floodwall mural of the gaseous diffusion plant.

Robert Dafford floodwall mural of traffic going to the gaseous diffusion plant in Paducah.

marked the boundary between North Korea and China. On November 26, Chinese armies marched south, and the conflict entered a new phase. The need for additional atomic bombs to cope with the anticipated hordes of humans attacking in endless waves put more emphasis on hurrying the location of a new atomic plant. On November 27, the AEC made a final decision to go ahead with a gaseous diffusion plant in Paducah.[277]

Paducah experienced shifts in population following the flood of 1937. Areas within the city emptied as people sought higher ground in the west end. Avondale Heights, Colonial Heights, Afton Heights and Arcadia attracted the more affluent. As a consequence, there was surplus residential space in the city limits. Soon, Paducahans realized that all such space would be needed and more.[278]

The presence of the hydroelectric generating plant of the TVA at Kentucky Dam also influenced the decision of the AEC to pick Paducah for its new plant; however, the dam was not capable of generating sufficient firm power to meet the anticipated demands of the AEC. On December 16, 1950, TVA announced plans to build a coal-fired steam-generating plan with four units near Paducah.[279] Further, the AEC sought 850,000 kilowatts of steam power to supply the energy needed to produce the enriched uranium, and the TVA plant could supply only half that. Five private utilities combined to create a new corporation known as Electric Energy Incorporated (EEI), which would supply the remainder. The TVA plant was called the Shawnee Steam Plant and was located next to the AEC; the EEl generators were located in Joppa, Illinois, just over the Ohio River. Estimated workers on the three projects ran over twenty thousand early in 1951. Paducah began to fill up.[280]

Housing shortages caused many Paducahans to rent their extra rooms. "Before 1950, a good sleeping room could be rented for four or five dollars a week. This soon rose to $10 and, later, the better locations were getting $15 a week. Finally, on October 17, 1951, the government ordered rent control."[281] Gradually, existing space was taken. Still more workers arrived. Temporary building met the demand for a time. Eventually, the delays in constructing additional housing were resolved, and the city overbuilt. Forest Hills contained 500 units; Fair Oaks had 120; California Court, 76; and the Paducah Apartments, 70. Most of these were completed after the boom passed. Previously, 300 apartments had been built at Elmwood Court, 100 at Anderson Court and 162 homes in River Oaks subdivision. Black Oaks provided 60 more units.[282]

Much of the floating population was located outside the city. Trailer parks sprang up everywhere in the county. Flattop Village came into being near the plant; later, the name changed to Forrestdale. Over 1,500 residents moved in. Dormitory-type buildings at the plant sites housed single construction workers.[283]

Private construction increased to meet the increased demand for housing. "Records in the office of the city building inspector show that 148 houses were started in 1950." William Ray Mofield, in his master's thesis, "The Atomic Age Comes to Paducah," notes that this was up slightly over the average, perhaps reflecting an increase toward the end of the year after the news of the new plant had been released. "In 1951, the number climbed to 476 and the figure leaped to an astronomical 741 in 1952." The peak had passed; however, construction continued to be above normal. In 1953, there were 285 starts; in 1954, 129; in 1955, 111; and by 1956, only 95.[284] Construction within the city put pressure on existing sewers and on the water lines.

The location of the three plants near Paducah had a tremendous impact on the business district of the city. "Shoppers were so thick in the stores it often took an hour just to get the attention of a clerk," Mofield notes. "Many customers walked away in disgust." Another facet to the influx of workers was the upward pressure on wages for clerks. "Retail stores were harassed by losing many of their experienced clerks too as hundreds flocked to the AEC area to take high paying jobs. Clerks who earned $40 soon found they could make $100 a week or more, and the rush was on." Lack of personnel reduced the ability of the stores to serve the increasing demand with traditional working hours. According to Mofield, "By February 3, 1951, it was evident the stores could not possibly handle the crowds in the number of hours they were operating, so on that date, the Retail Merchants Association voted to stay open Wednesday night each week until 8:30 instead of closing at the traditional 5:00 P.M." Protests from prayer meeting people forced the merchants to change from Wednesdays to Fridays even though it meant working on the Sabbath.[285] Habits changed. Mofield points out that there was little increase in the number of retail establishments in Paducah. Surplus capacity accounts for part of the explanation. "There were no new shoe stores, or ladies' or men's clothing store built during this period." Mofield reported that one new department store "made its bow" during this period. In fact, "as far as the downtown business were concerned, only a few appliance and loan offices were inaugurated." Some expansion did take place out of the downtown area. "Cardinal Point, a million dollar shopping center of eight relatively small stores, was built at 28th and Cairo Road, and many front lawns became used car lots. That was about the extent of the new business as such."[286]

A great number of "shabby roadside markets covered every road leading out of the city. Five new drive-in movie theaters were built in the area, and the four downtown theaters were jammed day and night. Strangely enough, only one new night club was built in the city although there was only one in town when the boom started." Paducah attracted national attention during this period with its traffic jams. Hordes of people flocked into the downtown area, looking for something to do. Traffic flow became a major headache to the city.[287]

Mayor Robert Cherry faced problems much like those of Sauner and Fisher during the Civil War. Paducah was overflowing with outsiders, and the boomers were not restricted by military discipline. Criminals might try to exploit the relative weakness of the Paducah police force, but first, something had to be done to handle the increased traffic. A separate traffic department was established with a captain, a lieutenant, a sergeant and twelve patrol officers out of the total forty-eight men on the force. Thirteen new officers were employed, and an auxiliary force was organized to help with traffic flow. Mayor Cherry also increased the budget for the police from $168,693.19 for 1951 to $199,648.11 in 1952. Additional increases were made in 1953 to a total of $245,928.42. As a result, there were no insurmountable traffic problems or significant increase in crime. Cherry helped reduce the traffic congestion by diverting the flow. Both Broadway and Jefferson were made one-way streets to alleviate the bottleneck in the downtown area. As for crime, a comparison of the police blotter for 1950 with that of 1953 is as follows:[288]

	1950	1953
Arrests	3,822	7,379
Murders	0	8
Assault	27	103
Sex Offenses	9	18
Common Drunkenness	2,279	3,494
Disorderly Conduct	231	577
Drunk Driving	181	326
Speeding	141	764
Running Stop Signs	137	645
Accidents	796	1,534
Injuries	104	252
Deaths	0	4

Robert Mills, the first professional architect born in the United States designed this fifty-bed hospital. Louisville had a one-hundred-bed structure. Mills also designed the Washington Monument in the District of Columbia. The Paducah building burned in 1863, and Fort Anderson was built there to defend the city from Confederates. Nathan B. Forrest attacked the post in 1864, but the assault failed.

The crime rate dropped noticeably after 1954.

The influx of population put a serious strain on hospital space in Paducah. Riverside and the Illinois Central Hospitals were near capacity without the additional load. The Baptists rushed construction of a new facility, starting building in 1951 and opening in late 1953.[289]

Next to housing, the greatest shortage produced by the boom was in school accommodations. "By a stroke of luck, Paducah was well prepared with plans. Dr. Mark Scully, the superintendent of schools, had just finished work on his doctor's degree from Columbia University's Teachers College by writing a dissertation on how to expand the Paducah school system."[290] Planning was needed. Enrollment in 1950 was 4,930; by early 1951, an additional 300 students had to be handled. In 1952, the city schools had to provide for 5,747 children without any additional funds (no government funding was available to assist the school system until 1953). The highest point in the enrollment cycle was reached in 1953, with 6,337 students, and 1954 had a reduction of only 3 students.[291]

The only way to raise the money needed to build new schools was by putting the bond issue on the ballot in a general election. Mofield notes, "The city began building its new high school plant, but it was not completed until 1955, and formal dedication of the new $3,000,000 building did not come until June 3, 1956." All money for the project came from local sources. "When federal funds were finally given in 1953, they were used to build a new addition at Brazelton Junior High...including eight classrooms, cafeteria, and auditorium-gymnasium; Clark school got... nine classrooms, a cafeteria and kitchen; and Jackson...built five new classrooms, a kitchen, and a heating plant." In addition, federal funds provided two-thirds of the money for Northside, which replaced three outmoded schools. Forest Hills School was built entirely with federal funds. Local monies also improved Morgan, McKinley, Jefferson and Lincoln High Schools.[292]

Mayor Cherry insisted that the growth of the city must be orderly. The city had passed a planning and zoning ordinance in 1928, but this merely identified the business and manufacturing districts at the time. All other property was declared residential. A full-time executive secretary was hired for the planning board (Thomas Burleigh), and the services of a professional planning consultant were secured (Kenneth Shellie Associates of Indianapolis, Indiana). The city commission passed an interim zoning plan that served until the master plan was completed about a year later.[293]

The city of Paducah was hard pressed to supply the increased water demand imposed by the rapid population growth. A water shortage developed in the summer of 1951 and continued into 1952. Mayor Cherry called a halt to washing automobiles and the watering of lawns. The local system had to expanded. The city commission gave the water board permission to issue $750,000 in revenue bonds, and $500,000 were issued in April 1952. Immediately, steps were taken to expand the plant, which had been built in 1885. The capacity of the system was almost doubled by local effort.[294]

Sewage treatment also proved to be a problem. Paducah paid for its own treatment plant via a bond issue. The new plant was dedicated on November 3, 1957.[295] Had the city waited, federal help would have been available. In 1956, Congress passed a law to permit payment of half the cost of sewage treatment plants required by participants in the Ohio Valley Sanitation Compact.[296]

Paducah managed to meet the challenge of the boom connected with the construction of the AEC plant and the two related steam-generating plants without outside aid. Cherry, like Hazelip in the flood of 1913, exemplified self-reliance. The city even managed to provide recreation sufficient to handle a doubled population. In 1952, Cherry had William Hay of the National Recreation Association survey Paducah. Hay said that the city needed 520 acres of parks for a population of sixty-five thousand, but nothing was done due to a lack of funding; however, existing parks were improved with baseball and softball diamonds and tennis courts. A full-time recreation director was employed to better utilize the existing parks. The Concert Association could not increase membership since it was limited by a 1,850-seat auditorium. People made do with what was available.[297]

The boom did not bring a great rush of industry to the Paducah area; one would think that it would have. Instead, the Paducah area acquired an image that only now is it able to forget. As Mofield notes, "Labor troubles brought Paducah unwillingly into the national spotlight time and again. The strikes were frequent and exasperating, especially to the Association of Commerce which was trying…to sell the Paducah–Calvert City area as the ideal place for new industry to locate."[298] What sold was the image of Paducah as a center of controversy. Articles in *Business Week*, *Time*, *U.S. News and World Report*, *Collier's* and other national magazines helped perpetuate the image of Paducah as being a poor risk for new investment. National attention did not prove to be beneficial. Nor was such an image justified.[299]

The number of strikes is disputed because "management and labor would never reveal the number on the various subcontracting firms and at Shawnee and Joppa. A list was kept by Bill Powell, city editor of the *Sun-Democrat*, from the strikes that got into print. He came up with a total of 84."[300] Despite the number, the plant was completed ahead of schedule. Furthermore, the project came in under cost estimates.[301]

As the labor-management rift widened, the city administration tried to provide some means of settling such disputes short of a walk-out. Mayor Cherry appointed a group that was available to arbitrate disputes. Dr. Robert Gordon Matheson, dean of Paducah Junior College, served as chairman. No one on the committee had previous experience in such proceedings, but they were willing. The program proved to be effective. Dean Matheson was selected to serve on the American Arbitration Association as a result of his successful experiences in Paducah disputes. Many potential strikes were avoided.[302]

Chapter 10

FUN AND FROLIC

Entertainment in Paducah changed dramatically after the Civil War. True, Captain John Betts, his wife and his sister-in-law, Nancy Standard, built a two-story frame building on Broadway between First and Second Streets in 1834. The upper floor served as living quarters while the lower level was used to show comedies, popular farces and light dramas. Traveling companies began to make regular stops in the new river community.[303]

In 1860, the brick St. Clair Hall was built at 112–14 South Second Street between Broadway and Kentucky, facing the Market. This theater was named for Sallie St. Clair, a popular actress who frequently performed in Paducah. Following the Civil War, the location of the St. Clair fell out of favor with the population of the city, and the theater declined. The structure was demolished in 1895.[304]

The citizens of Paducah looked forward to a new era with the completion of Morton's Opera House. This building seated 1,100. An air of expectancy followed the periodic reports on the progress of the structure. Brickwork was finished on August 13, 1884. An announcement on September 26 indicated that the building soon would be ready. Finally, on November 10, Miss Patti Rose's Opera Company opened in *Mizpah*, with local talent providing the music for the performance. The rates charged are a measure of the importance Paducahans placed on the theater. Reserved seats went for one dollar; parquet and dress circle, seventy-five cents; balcony, fifty cents; and gallery, twenty-five cents. Typical of the offerings available at the theater would be Augustin Daly's *Under the Gas Light*, Wilson and Rankin's *Minstrels*

Art nook on Second Street.

and Eunice Goodrich and Company in *Zizi*, *Pearl of Savoy*, *Pocahontas* and *A Straw Man* in 1888.[305]

Not all performances at the city opera house were by professionals. *The Skeleton Witness* was performed by a cast that included Lorena Scott, Lula Watson, Annie Given and, from the Concordia Dramatic Club, Mrs. A.W. Williams, Mary Weille and Gertie Solomon. Male members of the cast came from the Bullitt Light Artillery Company, commanded by Captain Rhey Boyd.[306]

One of the most unusual performances to be seen at Morton's was that of *Uncle Tom's Cabin* in 1889. The one-night stand was augmented by a special attraction billed as a "Big Double Brass Band" and a "Grand Double Orchestra." What was so unusual was that both white and colored musicians participated together. Integration was only token, however.[307]

Fire claimed Morton's in 1900.[308] A new and grander theater replaced Morton's. The Kentucky Theater was built at a cost of $60,000 and could seat 1,600. The structure was located on north Fifth Street between Broadway and Jefferson Streets. The occasion of the grand opening was tinged with sadness. President McKinley died on September 14, and Paducah still mourned his assassination; nevertheless, the city planned a gala benefit for September 24, 1901. Tickets for the opening went high. Orchestra seats cost $5.00, as did the first five rows of the balcony. The rest of the balcony cost $3.00. The first three rows of the gallery sold for $2.00, and the remainder went for $1.50 each. Herbert Cawthorne and a troupe of eighty presented *The Burgomaster*, a play based on the biography of Peter Stuyvesant of New Amsterdam.[309]

After the opening, rates at the Kentucky Theater dropped dramatically. *Dad's Girl* and *On the Sahara* followed the opening performance.[310] Tickets for these comedies sold for twenty-five, thirty-five and fifty cents.

Over the years, many famous names appeared on the show bills at the theaters of Paducah. Lillian Russell, Otis Skinner, William Gillette, Lionel Barrymore, Eva Tanguay, Al G. Field's Minstrels, John Phillip Sousa and his world-famous band and others appeared at the Kentucky. The community took little note when the YMCA introduced an innovation in entertainment: the movies. Yet this mode of entertainment soon replaced the legitimate theater.[311]

The presence of good theaters in Paducah did more than just bring traveling troupes into the community. Live performances also allowed local talent an opportunity to learn stagecraft. Herbert Wallerstein wrote songs that were popular with the local community; "Mister Moon" was sung by the leading lady in the *Buster Brown* opera. The following April, Wallerstein's

Left: Second Street between Kentucky and Broadway.

Below: The corner of Second Street and Kentucky.

"Merry Mary" was played by Deal's orchestra at the new Kentucky Theater, while Henrietta Crossman appeared in *Contrary Mary*.[312]

Besides the theater, Paducahans enjoyed local entertainment. A grand musical was performed by the Germania Singing Society at Lehrer's Hall in 1874.[313] Parades, cornet bands and lodges counted for many bright moments in an otherwise drab period; however, the Hook and Ladder Company and the Paducah Silver Cornet Band had to postpone one parade due to muddy streets. The coming of the new street railroad made band concerts and excursions popular. A pinwheel and band concert was held at Bellevue Garden on July 4, 1877. The festive events were capped by a balloon ascent. Beer, ice cream and the music of James Fitch's string band kept the crowd happy.[314]

Among the Episcopalians, musical gatherings and ice cream socials were frequent in the 1870s and 1880s to raise money to pay for the new Grace Church building. In a letter from Frannie Rabb to her sister Mary on February 2, 1873, Frannie reported that "Mr. Leopold's concert and Mrs. Pickett's charade came off in both of which I take part. The charade is for the benefit [of] the church parish Aid Society. It is going to be in Mrs. Pickett's parlour. She herself is going to recite a piece." Frannie wished she could prevail on Mrs. Pickett to dance the Highland fling.[315]

If Mrs. James Thomas Pickett, wife of the rector, did not consent to do the fling, perhaps her daughter did. At least May Pickett contributed to the efforts of the members of Grace Church to pay for their building. In May Pickett's diary for July 8, 1875, she notes, "There is a great deal of fun in Kentucky moonlight picnics for the benefit of the different denominations. They are all the rage."[316] She continued, "Our church had an elegant one last night in Mrs. McClelland's yard. The piano was on the porch and we had music everywhere we went."[317]

An entry in the diary for July 17, 1875, recorded another fundraiser attended by May Pickett: "Had a very nice time last night. The ice-cream was all sold early. Mrs. George Langstaff had lemonade and sherbet on one side of the yard and Miss Gus put her table and ice-cream on the other side. $24.50 was made."[318]

Sometimes, the socials were organized by business firms to foster sales. An advertisement in the *Paducah Daily News* of May 28, 1879, on page one, announced that Mrs. Harris, the proprietor of the Mineral Well, would give a moonlight party on the following evening for "young ladies and gentlemen only." Croquet was in vogue for the active. The two swings were available for cozy conversations. Strawberries and ice cream would be served to all.

Among the Germans, weddings provided occasions for festivities. For example, on July 5, 1879, Conrad Beyer married Katie Lehrer in the German Lutheran Church (St. Paul's). Reverend John Ansorge performed the ceremony at 8:00 p.m. The party moved to the residence of Henry Diehl for supper. At 10:00 p.m., the Plain City string band began playing for dancing "until the wee hours."[319]

Steamboat cruises were also popular in the period. During the summer of 1879, one could ride from Paducah to Cairo on the *James Fisk Jr.* or the *Champion* and return, eat two meals and pay only a quarter.[320]

Young boys had different ideas of entertainment. The slow-moving streetcars were objects of pranks on more than one occasion. Bricks were placed on the tracks on Locust Street (now Third Street). The driver did not see them and was thrown over the front of the car. Fortunately for him, the car did not run up on him, nor did the mule express his objection to the new arrangement. Nevertheless, Pat Halloran, manager of the line, expressed concern and urged parents to discourage the practice. A similar prank took place on Broadway in front of the American German National Bank nine years later. A railroad signal torpedo was placed on the car tracks and went undetected until the car passed over it. The resulting explosion caused the driver and passengers to tumble out of the car while the employees of the bank, thinking they were being attacked, appeared at the door with cocked pistols. One bystander commented that he was reminded of Forrest's raid.[321]

Much of the entertainment in Paducah was generated in the home. The piano became the center of family musical gatherings (at least until the 1937 flood). Music lessons were a must for the proper Paducahan. An advertisement dated September 15 appeared in the local paper on August 1 and again on August 22, 1879, announcing that Miss Purington planned to resume teaching in September. Mr. V. Eisenman offered voice lessons and instrumental instruction at the same time. Twenty weeks of instruction in a class of two cost twenty-five dollars; thirty dollars for private lessons.[322] For those not able to generate music from a pump organ or piano, the player piano and the Edison phonograph proved to be a boon. Mrs. C.L. Rieke put her new Edison phonograph on public display and then invited a select group to a private party that featured Italian and American opera, band and orchestra selections. She also had one cylinder of literary recitations.[323]

If one wished, candies, sweetmeats and luxury foods were available in Paducah from Julius Weil and Company. Cream pecans; marshmallow pellets; Grecian almonds; Baby Alligators; fruits, fresh and dried; clams;

oysters from New Orleans and Baltimore; soda drinks; novelties and party favors; China sardines—the list goes on and on. The firm did regular business with St. Louis, Chicago, Nashville, Evansville, New York City, Louisville, Memphis, New Orleans, Mobile, Cincinnati, Baltimore, Kalamazoo, Atlanta, Philadelphia and Durham. Boston and Indianapolis sent items on regular consignment, as did Detroit. Paducah might have been small, but it was not isolated. Situated as it was on both rail and water trade routes, Paducahans could have the best of everything.[324]

Mary Flournoy Boswell and her sister kept a scrapbook during the 1870s, 1880s and 1890s that illustrates the social life of popular, young, well-to-do debutantes in Paducah. The popular dance of the period was the "German." The Palmer House was the center of much of the social life of the community during this period, and dances were held in the hotel's ballroom. The young people coined names for themselves. The Debutante Club, the Original Eighteen, the Metropolitan Club, the Kenton Klub and the Cinque Club were but a few whose invitations appear in the book. One example was the card from the first German of the German Club and the Cinque Club at the Elks' Hall on October 21, 1869.[325]

Art also attracted a following in Paducah—especially when it depicted ladies in their next-to-nothings. A display of lithographs in show windows on Broadway in 1889 induced an outburst of displeasure. Needless to say, the raffle of an oil painting of the riverfront by Walter Seis did not warrant equal coverage in the same paper.[326]

The arrival of a circus was occasion for celebration—most of the time. Smith's Great American Circus played Paducah in 1857. Dan Rice appeared in the city in 1870. John Robinson set up his show on the Bynd property on south Third Street and played to an estimated three thousand patrons one afternoon in 1888. However, the *Buffalo Bill Wild West Show* seemed to have hit a particularly responsive chord in Paducah. Opening on November 19, 1884, the cowboy show was an immediate hit. Large crowds pressed forward to watch the daring riders; youth in the town tried to imitate the heroes of the West. Buffalo Bill returned to Paducah on more than one occasion. In fact, Paducah became the home of a rival to the show of Mr. Bill Cody. Fletcher Terrell created the *Buckskin Bill Wild West Show*, which claimed to be surpassed only by the Cody show and that of Pawnee Bill. Wagons and equipment of the troupe wintered in Paducah and vicinity.[327]

By 1905, Paducah was an established convention city. The Elks, the state gun clubs, various church convocations and others enjoyed the open hospitality of the city. In August of that year, the city had two large groups to converge on it at the same time, straining accommodations to their limit. An army training camp brought in a wave of young men. Even Governor J.C.W. Beckham visited Camp Yeiser to inspect the Second Kentucky Regiment.[328] Fear of yellow fever made it uncertain until the last moment whether Paducah would be able to handle the additional population. In fact, the city health officials and Mayor Yeiser differed on whether to issue quarantine. The prospect of added revenue loomed large in the insistence that the city remain open. Better to remove the health officers than to close the city. The soldiers were welcomed.[329]

The second large group to descend on Paducah that summer arrived on August 8. "From all parts of Tennessee, Kentucky, Indiana, and Illinois have Negroes assembled here to carry out the annual celebration of August 8." The field at Wallace Park was tacitly reserved for the masses who arrived on special trains from Louisville, St. Louis, Memphis, Hopkinsville and Evansville. Ben Boyd's Nationals, a baseball team composed of blacks from the Paducah area, played a visiting team. Picnic lunches and lighthearted revelry marked the occasion. Thousands enjoyed the celebration.[330] This event is still observed, but most have forgotten the origin.

Paducah has been threatened by outside forces on several occasions—invasion by rival armies, cholera, yellow fever and riders from the Black Patch. The latter refers to a region of Kentucky and Tennessee that produces dark-fired tobacco. Essentially, there are four divisions to the Black Patch: the Northern, with markets in Owensboro, Henderson and Madisonville; the Eastern, with markets in Hopkinsville, Princeton and Clarksville and Springfield, Tennessee; the Western, with markets in Mayfield, Murray, Fulton and Paducah and Paris, Tennessee; and the Bowling Green One-Sucker District, with sales at Bowling Green, Glascow and Horse Cave. By the end of the nineteenth century, Duke's American Tobacco Trust was trying to gain domination for dark-fired tobacco in the domestic market. Two rival groups emerged in the Black Patch: the Hill Billies, who went along with the trust, and the Night Riders, who banded together in an attempt to gain a better price for their product from the trust. All that was necessary to be a Night Rider was a horse, a mask and an alibi. Princeton, Hopkinsville and Clarksville were occupied by armed bands of Night Riders. Warehouses of the trust were burned at Princeton and Hopkinsville. Anyone opposing the secret army was subjected to terror; if a grower, his plant bed would be "scalped" to ensure that no crop would be grown, and on occasion, the person of a Hill Billie would be violated. A pact of silence ensured that anyone tried for Night Riding would be freed by a jury of his peers. All of western Kentucky watched the conflict with both dread and admiration. "Even in such a place as Paducah…reports of preparation for the raiding of the city by Night Riders had been received, and serious, well-grounded apprehension was felt for the safety of the large tobacco warehouses there."[331]

Robert Hollowell and his wife, Mary Lou, had been raided by Night Riders at their home near Princeton. In the affair, Mrs. Hollowell had been injured by gunfire. A Caldwell County jury freed those accused of the attack. The Hollowells left Kentucky and moved to Evansville. There they entered suit against the Night Riders in the federal district court in Paducah. Many feared that the Night Riders might use force to prevent the trial or to intimidate the witnesses. "While the more prominent court officials and the leading business people of Paducah were opposed to the Night Riders and in sympathy with our clients," wrote Jim Miller, "we learned for a certainty that there was in considerable classes a strong undercurrent to the contrary, and in communities within easy striking distance there were organizations that might well be feared."[332] Paducahans watched the coming trial with a sense of both dread and fascination.

On April 22, 1908, the trial of Robert Hollowell versus his brother, John E. Hollowell, and twenty-seven other accused Night Riders began. The testimony was characterized as being sensational, yet nothing new was introduced from the previous trial in the state court. Arguments were completed on April 23. Judge Walter Evans instructed the jury: W.E. Cochran George Langstaff, Major T.H. Ashcraft and James Kroger of Paducah; W.A. Lawrence of Graves County; W.A. Gresham of Lyon County; and W.F. Cherry of Carlisle County. The following day, the paper reported that the jury deadlocked after seven hours. Gresham and Cherry were for acquittal; the rest found for Robert Hollowell. Judge Evans dismissed the jury.[333]

A new trial for the Night Riders began in May. To ensure that the jury would not be compromised again, a panel from Jefferson and Bullitt Counties, two hundred miles away, heard the case. The jury got the case late on May 13 and rendered its verdict on May 14. The Night Riders were fined $35,000 in damages. The Night Rider movement withered and died. A common reply of a farmer in Caldwell County to the query, "What are you doing?" was "Plowing corn for Mary Lou."[334]

Sensational trials do not come along every day, but Paducahans liked to follow lurid stories in their newspapers. Moreover, when such tales were not available, the readers contented themselves with local events. The *Paducah Evening Sun* reported the results of a contest to determine the best-kept lawn in the city. Mrs. I.C. Flournoy took the ten-dollar first prize, and W.P. Paxton got an equal amount for the best-kept unimproved lot. Other winning cash prizes were George Goodman, Mrs. Louis Reike and Mrs. R.G. Terrell.[335]

A new era began in Paducah with the introduction of the automobile. The remarkable thing is that no one realized the impact of the new toy. In a short time, the very structure of the city changed. Firms catering to the horse faltered and failed. Patterns of living changed; people became more mobile. More surfaced roads led to a shift in centers of population from areas near the central business district to the suburbs. However, such changes were scarcely contemplated when Dr. J.D. Robertson accepted delivery of an Oldsmobile on November 2, 1901.[336] Other cars followed in rapid succession. On June 14, 1904, a shipment of Fords arrived at Foreman Brothers and made front-page news. Increasing use of the new vehicle quickly led to abuse.[337]

The city of Paducah reacted to the presence of the automobile by enacting an ordinance requiring all cars to have bells and lights. The speed was limited to eight miles per hour. Violation of the ordinance led to fines ranging from five to fifty dollars.[338] More powerful engines made the new machine more attractive. Soon, the small cars surpassed the twelve-horsepower capability of the electric streetcars of the time. No longer was man tied to steel rails; he was free to seek adventure on the open road.

Patrons of Paducah's papers liked to keep track of those saved from the clutches of madams. A young girl from the Cumberland River country arrived on a frigid morning in February 1879 and told a hack driver to take her to a house where she could make a living. She was saved from a "fate worse than death."[339] A similar report occurred in 1895. Cora Porter, sixteen years of age from Hardin County, Tennessee, was rescued from an evil drummer who had taken her to Anna Sanderson's on West Court Street. Cora was returned to her family. Then there was the strange account of Mrs. J.A. Elliot of south Ninth Street. On December 12, 1896, Mrs. Elliot went to the market to buy a hog's head. She was not heard from for two days. When she returned, Mrs. Elliot claimed that she had been looking for "second feet" shoes (used shoes). Someone told her of a place on south Tenth Street that sold used shoes. Mrs. Elliot wound up at Lou Howe's "resort" near the Chambliss brickyard. She claimed she was forced into a room with "a lantern jawed railroad man" for the entire time. The story was questioned, as Mrs. Elliot could not explain how she managed to get her hair shingled during the period she allegedly had been held captive.[340]

Occasionally, the police raided some of the bawdy houses. On June 29, 1883, the *Daily News* reported a raid of the "Frenchtown nymphs," and fines ranging from twenty-five to forty dollars were awarded the "girls." Perhaps the proper citizens were right in their belief that the "girls" were at the very nadir of degradation. At least the case of Lottie Edwards indicated that the retirement benefits of the profession left much to be desired. Lottie died in Madam Seitz's in August, and the city paid for her pauper's grave. Business must have been bad or competition must have been fierce. Seven houses were reported operating in April of that year.[341]

In 1903, a major effort to close the bawdy houses in Paducah came from the ministerial association. The city was booming. A total of twenty-nine building permits were issued in April alone.[342] Many conventions met in Paducah that year. Religious revivals stirred interest in reform. On June 3, the ministerial association issued a challenge to the city authorities to clean up corruption in the community. The charge was that 350 immoral women inhabited Paducah. The physicians were quoted as saying that the lewd women "caught" 90 percent of the young men in the area. There were no major incidents in Paducah.[343]

After a flood and a homecoming, Paducah again tackled the problem of prostitution. The leader of this movement was Clinton S. Quin, the new rector of Grace Episcopal Church. In one of the fifty-seven diaries kept by Quin, he described Paducah as being "like ancient Damascus, and Sodom and Gomorrah." To Quin, the city "was a trading city, the host of countless drummers and, therefore, the provender of appropriate entertainment."[344]

The reform movement gained momentum slowly. In 1916, a vice commission was appointed, with Quin as chairman. Its report made specific recommendations for the reform of morality in Paducah. Enforcement of existing laws against prostitution, punchboards and gambling was the key in the program to reform Paducah. Reform began on July 24, when Chief Henley Franklin was demoted to patrolman and replaced by James W. Eaker.[345] Two days later, the papers reported that city hall was calm again and that the vice commission was hopeful that effective action would take place against the notorious houses.[346] On July 27, Eaker and his men made visits to every known house and informed them that they would have to comply with the law.[347]

The mayor, Ernest Lackey, felt that something must be done for the inhabitants of the houses. Lackey suggested that a temporary home be secured for the girls. To that end, the city secured the use of 333 South Second Street. Later, a special section of Riverside Hospital was made available to treat diseased prostitutes.[348]

Many in the community felt that the officials were dragging their feet in the closing of the houses. Judge C.B. Crossland made hints at a "whiskey ring protecting the prostitutes and criticized city officials."[349] Finally, the city adopted the thirty-two final clauses suggested by the vice commission on August 15. The work of the commission was at an end; it remained for the city to enforce the program of reform.[350]

On September 5, the city appointed a morals commission. Members of this new organization were Sanders E. Clay, commissioner of public safety; Reverend Clinton S. Quin; Dr. Vernon Blythe; Andrew Nichols, an attorney; and Rabbi Lee. J. Levinger.[351] The group was to oversee the community. A statement of purpose for the morals commission appeared on September 12. The group planned to supervise all commercialized forms of recreation in Paducah.[352]

The deadline came without any rash of arrests. Nine new patients did appear at the VD clinic at Riverside Hospital. Many felt cheated. The vice commission had identified 174 women as prostitutes, yet no arrests were made on September 19, 20 or 21. People began to wonder why. In fact, a grand jury began to take evidence on the closing of the houses on October 12. A week later, Judge Crossland insisted that the houses were still operating.[353] The question of whether the houses were operating spilled over into the election of members to the city commission.

On October 20, Crossland claimed that Sanders Clay was encouraging the police to slow down the closing of the houses. Three affidavits were filed to show that Clay and Mayor Lackey permitted houses to operate if player pianos were kept quiet and no porch lights burned. In addition to the affidavit of Crossland, Patrolman Vick of the "Gash" District and Emma Martin, a madam, filed affidavits to affirm Crossland's charge. These charges came just before the primary election. Both Lackey and Clay lost the primary. Lackey had been elected for a four-year term, but due to the dispute with Frank Burns, his election had been challenged in

Riverside Hospital, 1913.

court. A new election went to Burns, and the houses closed—at least for a while.[354]

Between the great reform effort of 1916 and the present, prostitution in Paducah has kept a low profile. One or two houses continued to provide for community needs and were tolerated. During the boom in the early 1950s and into the early 1960s, Paducah gained the reputation of being a good liberty town for servicemen, especially from Fort Campbell. City leaders encouraged this image.

As Paducah entered the 1980s, opportunities for entertainment increased. Paducah Community College offered a continuing program in community education and entertainment. The Lillian Lowry Focus series in the performing arts paralleled that of the community concert series and broadened cultural opportunities for the city. In addition, the Market House Theatre restored the legitimate theater in Paducah. Offerings included tried and tested plays plus new works, including that of local authors such as Dr. Ben Bradford. Short programs and forums were available through the city recreation program, local churches and the City-County Arts Council. The city even had a symphony orchestra that supplemented musical performances by the various schools. Tilghman

Fort Campbell personnel drop in on the Festival on the River in Paducah.

had an established reputation in musicals that built on the excellent training available in choral music from elementary through twelfth grade in the city schools. The college also supported a Community Chorus that presented at least two concerts per year. Cultural programs were available to the community via Channel 2 on the cable TV system. The Boys Choir exchanged a visit with the world-famous Vienna Boys Choir and was favorably received.

The new Jackson House senior citizens' center, 1980.

Market House Theatre.

The Summer Festival, started by Mayor Tom Wilson, gives the city a variety of entertainment, ranging from street bands to the masters of classical music. Even *National Geographic* took notice of this annual event in June 1973. Paducahans should be proud.

Chapter 11

BENDING THE COLOR LINE

In 1948, Harry Truman did more for equal rights with the stroke of a pen than any president since the passage of the Fifteenth Amendment. The armed forces were desegregated by executive order. Hope of equality of opportunity was realized, at least in one small segment of American life. Pressure for further gains mounted.

"Free by '63" became the call of the black community. One hundred years after the signing of the Emancipation Proclamation, many black Americans still lacked social and political equality. Young blacks had opened the decade of the '60s with a new type of protest: "On February l, 1960, four students from the Negro Agricultural and Technical College in Greensboro, North Carolina entered a variety store, made several purchases, and then sat down at the lunch counter and ordered coffee."[355] Thus began the black revolution of the 1960s. Imitating the passive resistance used successfully in South Africa by Mohandas Gandhi, the "sit-in" movement started the first crack in the wall of legal segregation. Gains were met at great cost to many in the movement.

Conditions in Paducah were not dissimilar from those in the nation. Between 1872 and 1916, the black man was courted for his vote and relegated to second-class status as a citizen. On October 23, 1883, "a colored barber" tried to sit in the section reserved for whites in the St. Clair Hall. He was ejected, to the delight of the local paper.[356]

Newspapers frequently objected to the boisterous behavior of bootblacks on Broadway. The issue for October 28, 1889, branded these blacks as "young hoodlums" and urged city authorities to run them out. A previous issue had reported that daughters of whites were offended by the "ribald and obscene" language of the bootblacks and "couldn't shop" as a result.[357]

Paducahans could be proud of accomplishments by local blacks; however, it was a patronizing pride. Henry H. Urquhart got paid $9,000 for a patent on a brake shoe for steam engines in 1905. At the time, Urquhart worked as a switchman on the Illinois Central.[358]

Race relations in Paducah reached their lowest point in 1916. Luther Durrett and Brack Kinley were lynched on October 16. Kinley was accused of raping a white woman on the Pool Road and had been put into county jail. A mob gathered and, despite the brave and determined resistance of Judge William Reed, took Kinley from the jail. Durrett followed the crowd, armed with a pistol and muttering threats to the mobs of whites. Durrett was seized and forced to go along to the house of the woman involved. There, Kinley was identified, and both blacks were hanged, shot and, at the hysterical insistence of Mrs. George D. Rose, burned. Five thousand people were said to have witnessed the event.[359]

Judge Reed branded the lynch mob murders and called for a special grand jury to investigate the incident. For his effort, Reed received the commendation of Governor A.O. Stanley and a warning note. On the same date that Governor Stanley sent his supporting letter to Reed, seventy-five blacks left Paducah. They went to West Virginia to work on the B&O Railroad. There is no evidence to prove that the lynching influenced the decision for so many blacks to migrate, but it might have influenced some.[360]

Curlee Brown, president of the Paducah Chapter of the NAACP, reported in an interview with Glen Murrell in 1967 that the organization decided to take action against Paducah Junior College (PJC) in 1948. The college was publically supported and was subject to the provisions of the Day Law prohibiting mixing of the races in schools.[361]

On September 12, 1949, Joseph S. Freeland, attorney for the NAACP in Paducah, and Lee Powell appeared at PJC seeking admission. Powell's credentials were examined by Dean Matheson, and his request for admission was denied—not for race but for scholarship.[362]

The following day, Freeland reappeared with Fred A. Wilson Jr. The college authorities had no recourse but to accept the application or obey the law. Wilson was refused admission because of his race. As a result, a suit was filed in the U.S. District Court for Western Kentucky at Paducah.[363]

The local legal staff of the NAACP received valuable assistance in preparing the case from Thurgood Marshall (later associate justice of the U.S. Supreme Court) and Robert Carter of the NAACP's Legal Defense and

Education Funds, Inc. As a result, the city of Paducah was added to the suit as a defendant since it contributed tax monies to the college.[364]

After legal maneuvering, the NAACP decided to retreat from a direct attack on the Day Law and attempt to prove that the doctrine of "separate but equal" education was being violated in Paducah. West Kentucky Industrial College had originated in 1907, when D.H. Anderson moved the Negro normal school from Mayfield to Paducah. This school became the first institution of higher education in the city, providing black teachers with basic courses to qualify them to teach. The school also became the center of cultural and social activity in the black community. The college functioned as a normal school until 1938, when the higher education component was moved to Kentucky State College in Frankfort.

On October 27, 1950, Judge Roy Shelbourne ruled that "qualified colored students had the right to attend Paducah Junior College."[365] One immediate consequence of this ruling was that the University of Louisville opened its doors to blacks. The Day Law was modified in 1950 to allow coeducation of whites and blacks in public or private school above the high school level if comparable courses were not then available at Kentucky State in Frankfort. PJC appealed the decision and continued to refuse admission to blacks.

On January 22, 1952, a mandatory injunction was issued by the Federal Court in Paducah "enjoining and restraining the college from excluding qualified Negroes."[366] Again, PJC appealed.

The United States Court of Appeals for the Sixth Circuit at Cincinnati found against PJC on February 2, 1953. Further appeal by the college ended. On June 9, 1953, four Negroes enrolled at the college without incident. Integration had begun in Paducah.[367]

Paducah was more fortunate than other towns in Kentucky in that integration came without violence. The National Guard unit from Paducah was called into active duty to prevent trouble at Sturgis. The leadership of Paducah should be commended in its constructive approach to this issue. Both blacks and whites refrained from creating a crisis environment. The control over public opinion exercised by the Paxton family proved to be helpful in this connection. While not censoring the news, the papers and TV exercised restraint in how news was slanted, thus moderating the conditions that could have gotten out of hand.

One significant influence in promoting peaceful integration was the Non-Partisan League. Reverend W.G. Harvey wrote to Mayor Robert Cherry on February 28, 1963, protesting the continued presence of Jim Crow signs at local movie theaters. The letter concluded, "We believe that progress in a city depends on the progress in civil rights, and we need a combination of efforts to take care of this matter, for we would like to do this peacefully and religiously, and with [sit-ins] or [picket lines], and would not [like] to resort to the last.[368]

Harvey's letter was passed on to Robert P. Petter, a member of the Mayor's Committee on Human Rights. Petter wrote to Harvey on March 13 and reported:

> *I was told at our Committee meeting last night that the sign at the Arcade Theater had been removed. We ourselves did not speak to Mr. Keiler about the signs because there are negotiations going on regarding the de-segregation of the theaters and we felt the signs would take care of themselves once de-segregation was achieved.*[369]

The signs indicated separate sections based on race.

The Non-Partisan League sent out a special announcement: "After July 1, 1963, all persons, regardless of race, creed or color will have access to the South Twin Drive In Theater, and the Sunset Drive In Theater." The announcement also noted that "after Labor Day, all persons will have access to the Paducah Drive In Theater, and after October 3, 1963, all areas and facilities at the Columbia and Arcade Theaters will be available to all persons." The league felt that this was quite an accomplishment and asked that those who chose to take advantage of these recreational facilities should be on their best behavior.[370]

Restraint was shown by all concerned. In a letter to John W. Keiler dated June 27, Harvey said, "On behalf of the Non-Partisan League of the Greater Paducah Area, I am happy to inform you that we have not had any undue publicity in the papers as you requested." A copy of the special announcement was enclosed, referring to the suggestion about good behavior.[371]

The Non-Partisan League worked with city officials to improve the chances for employment of blacks in municipal jobs. The approach was low key but effective. Mayor Cherry wrote to the chairmen of the water and power boards suggesting that since blacks consisted of 16.7 percent of the population in the city, a similar ratio should exist in employment practices. The league thanked the mayor in a letter dated June 27.[372]

Blacks began to be appointed to important civic boards during the 1960s. Harvey, Wilbur Lee, W.C. Young and other young blacks in the city became recognized as Paducah leaders instead of important blacks. Mayor Tom Wilson named Harvey to the city housing commission, breaking a precedent that had kept all Paducah boards white. Harvey's nomination was approved unanimously by the board of commissioners.[373]

The appointment of Harvey to fill a vacancy on the city board of commissioners by Mayor Robert Cherry also broke another color line. Harvey had been the runner-up in the election, losing by a narrow margin. An equally significant date was reported by George Chancellor in "Harvey Conducts Commission Meet" in the *Paducah Sun-Democrat*: "Saying simply, 'Would you call the roll, please?' The Rev. W.G. Harvey, a Negro, convened the first meeting of the Paducah City Commission to be presided over by a member of his race Tuesday night."[374] Wilbur Lee, the lone Negro on the Paducah Planning and Zoning Commission, expressed the sentiments of the black community on the history-making occasion: "I'm a proud black Paducahan tonight."[375]

The color line still exists, but it has been bent. Significant gains have been made, though much remains to be done. The remarkable thing is that the community could work out divisive problems without critical crises developing. Paducah should be both thankful and proud.

Chapter 12

UPDATE, 1980–2014

The epilogue of the previous issue of this history of Paducah ended with the advent of the Executive Inn convention center and the bending of the racial color line in the community: "Paducah is making a practical effort to keep its identity as a river city in the age of the automobile. It remains to see if the future population movements parallel Paducah planning. I think it will; I am positive on Paducah." Now, the community faces a plethora of crises. Its largest employer, the Paducah Gaseous Diffusion Plant, is laying off most of its workers; the Illinois Central Railroad, one of the largest employers in the commonwealth of Kentucky, is no more, replaced by the Paducah and Louisville (P&L) line; and the downtown Executive Inn is a memory. The Paducah city school system leads Kentucky in the ratio of black students to white students. Tilghman High School maintains its excellent sports reputation, but the aura of the old all-white Augusta Tilghman School is fading. McCracken County now has a new consolidated high school rather than continuing as Reidland, Lone Oak and Heath.

The art of quilting annually attracts thousands to Paducah. The National Quilt Museum at 215 Jefferson Street is one of the most important agents of change in downtown Paducah. Frank Bennett, CEO, wrote in the *Arts* January–February 2013 issue:

> *Every day people travel thousands of miles to visit Paducah. They are travelling to visit the largest tourist attraction in Western Kentucky. The destination they seek has won numerous national awards, including the Trip*

Paducah's Quilt Museum.

> *Advisor "Certificate of Excellence" and The Kentucky Governors Award in the Arts and is on most national "Must See Museum" lists. It has been mentioned in dozens of respected publications including* Southern Living *Magazine,* Forbes *Magazine, the* Wall Street Journal, *and The* Chicago Tribune. *In an average year, over 40,000 art enthusiasts from all 50 states and over 45 foreign countries come to Paducah to visit The National Quilt Museum making a significant cultural and economic impact on our community.*

Bennett goes on to say, "Many people in the community think the Quilt Museum is related to the AQS Quilt Show. I guess it's just because we're both involved with quilting, but we are actually as separate as Microsoft and Google. Our audiences are quite different too." The American Quilters Society show brings thousands of quilters to Paducah. "The museum [the world's largest] brings a more diverse audience that includes art enthusiasts, cultural tourists, and fiber artists."

In front of the Quilt Museum, a commemorative cluster of statues depicts Meriwether Lewis and William Clark en route to the Pacific Ocean in 1803. George Lundeen, the artist, included Seaman, the Newfoundland dog of Lewis, as well as representative Native Americans. Close inspection of the warrior's ear reveals a coin with the image of Sacagawea. The map in Clark's hand includes an error. Lundeen deliberately included a town at the junction of the Tennessee and Ohio Rivers named Paducah. In fact, the town was created in 1827 and named to honor a tribe of once-proud warriors in what is now Texas who were shattered by their neighbors, who received rifles from the Spanish and French. Clark explained to his son that he planned to change the spelling to make it easier for English-speaking people to pronounce. In

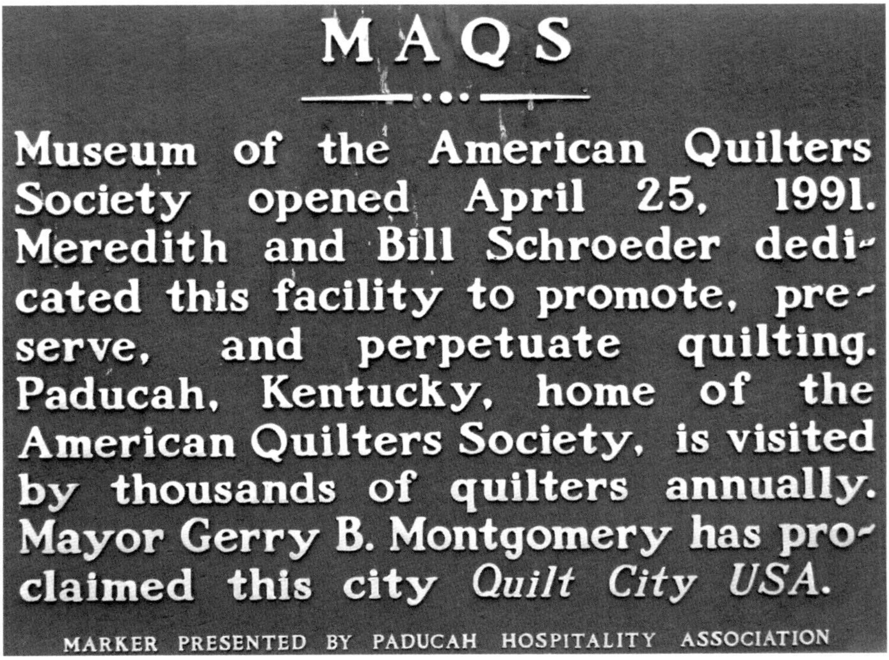

Museum of the American Quilters Society historical marker.

capital letters, Clark wrote, "PA DU CAH." Meriwether Lewis Clark, the son, was a fifteen-year-old cadet at West Point at the time. (The letter is in the Missouri Historical Society in St. Louis.)

The American Quilters Society show dominates life in Paducah for a short period every year with hordes of avid quilters cluttering streets and accommodations. This annual contest was brought to the community by Bill and Meredith Schroeder. Winning quilts in the annual event fetch prizes worth thousands of dollars. Owners of stalls in the mall and sites in the downtown district shift from their usual wares to focus on the needs of these guests. Unlike the Quilt Museum, this event is intense but brief. Afterward, the city sighs and settles back to welcome the rest of the year.

WKCTC (West Kentucky Community and Technical College, the former Southern Association–accredited Paducah Junior College) is among the five top community colleges in the nation. Finally, later in 2014, Murray State University will open its new branch in the city. Draughan's Business College is a memory, but other skill-based schools have emerged. The Seaman's

New Murray State University presence in Paducah.

West Kentucky Community and Technical College ranks fifth in the nation.

Church Institute nautical center now supplies computer-assisted simulation for mariners plying the inland waterways of the nation. Deep saltwater sailors are trained by this institution in Brooklyn, New York.

The Paducah Symphony Orchestra and chorus enliven the downtown Carson Center offerings. Founded in 1979, when local musicians performed in the annual Summer Festival, orchestra members were loath to abandon the group. Additional concerts were planned and performed on an ad hoc basis dependant on the funds raised. As subscription support grew, the symphony offered varied preplanned performances. Many concerts featured recognized artists. Dr. Jordan Tang directed the Paducah Symphony for twenty-three seasons, from 1987 to 2009, when Raffaele Pont assumed

Mariners on the inland waterways come to Paducah to receive computer-simulated training at the Seaman's Church Institute. This program can challenge the most senior mariner and requires instant reaction to avoid unexpected events. Candidates find themselves at the wheel of a mighty towboat with a tow of fifteen cantankerous heavy barges when a gust of wind hits from the starboard side. The experienced seamen say the simulation is daunting, as illustrated here by the floodwall mural by Robert Dafford showing the helmsman looking over his tow. The curriculum combines both perception and reaction. Safety afloat continues to be the primary target for training. Graduates can not only rise professionally but also rest more comfortably in knowing that they have gained experience without endangering others. These simulations have trained over 11,250 mariners from 1998 to 2012.

Paducah Seaman's Church Center for Maritime Education.

Carson Arts Center, home of the Paducah Symphony.

leadership of a group of seasoned artists with an operating budget that has expanded from $45,000 in 1981–82 to more than half a million dollars today. Orchestra members are all professionals from ten counties in western Kentucky and southern Illinois. Small ensembles regularly perform for schools and community and civic organizations each school year.

A handout from the orchestra notes:

> *The PSO's mission is to bring the rewards of great music to a growing and diverse regional audience. The PSO, presently the orchestra-in-residence at the Luther F. Carson Four Rivers Center, encompasses a wide range of ensembles, including the PSO Professional Orchestra, the Paducah POPS Orchestra, an auditioned adult Symphony Chorus, a multi-county Children's Chorus, and a Music Education Program. The Paducah Pops has performed at Kentucky Dam Village State Park…Marion, Hopkinsville, Marshall County High School, Winchester, Murray, Southeast Missouri State University and Southeast Illinois Community College.*

The orchestra has also performed several times for the Paducah Summer Festival, attracting audiences of ten to twelve thousand people. In 1994, the orchestra had the distinction of backing up the Moody Blues band in a concert at Cape Girardeau and vocalist Amy Grant at the Luther F. Carson Four Rivers Center (2007).

The symphony offers educational opportunities seldom seen in small communities such as Paducah:

> *Under the direction of Dr. Brad Almquist, head of the Choral Department at Murray State University, the adult chorus has gained an international reputation for moving audience members to tears. The group performs at least two programs per season with the Orchestra and also offers a cappella concerts. Dr. Almquist also conducts the Children's Chorus.*

The handout concludes

> *For over 30 years the PSO has served as the premier musical organization serving Western Kentucky and the surrounding region, expanding its appearances through collaborations with community partners and enhancing the area's cultural reputation. It is most unusual for a city Paducah's size to have an orchestra, much less a highly successful one.*

The Market House Theatre (MHT) celebrates its fiftieth anniversary in 2014. "In the fall of 1963, eight individuals made a formal decision to create a theatre group in Paducah," notes a pamphlet issued for the occasion. The goal of the group was to provide quality community theater productions that would be "excellent opportunities for education and experiences in the dramatic arts!" Located in the market building that now houses both the theater and a museum, a group of eight individuals met and formed the Market House Players. The *Paducah Sun* reviewed the first production, *The Male Animal*, in April 1964: "The spectators, many of whom came out of loyalty to the project, soon were carried away with the show. Loyalty soon turned to appreciation." This continues to characterize offerings of the Paducah Company, which now is a nationally recognized 501(c) (3) arts organization with awards from the American Association of Community Theatre, the Southeastern Theatre Conference and the Kentucky Theatre Association for "its outstanding performance quality and innovative educational programming. MHT is dedicated to showcasing the talent of community residents of Western Kentucky, Southern Illinois, Northwestern Tennessee, and Southeastern Missouri."

Currently, the MHT has a professionally trained staff that puts on five plays each year. For 2013, it offered *Godspell*, September 5–15, and *To Kill A Mockingbird*, October 31–November 10. For 2014, it will run the *Fox on the Fairway*, January 16–26; *Steel Magnolias*, April 17–27; and *Young Frankenstein*,

Market House. *Courtesy of the William Clark Museum.*

June 5–22. Recent attendance for these productions was eighteen thousand adults. Furthermore, the staff offers three plays in its Family Series with youth involved in production and presentation. A touring group, the Story Theatre, serves over thirty elementary and preschool audiences in the four-state region. Also, "creative drama classes at the theatre and in area schools provide arts education for more than 28,000 school children." For a city of its size, continued support of this theater in Paducah is remarkable.

The theater art program of the MHT is "accessible and affordable to everyone in our community." Effort is made to ensure that the offerings are economically feasible to the target audience:

> *Many of our classes offer scholarships, and opportunities exist for volunteers to see shows for free or at a reduced price. Volunteers are the core of MHT operations. Newcomers are welcomed to participate in all aspects of theatre operations. No experience is necessary—we provide the training!*

Artists moving into Lower Town have produced a vibrant core of urban renewal that now works its way westward into the Fountain Avenue area. Structures are preserved and improved. Many fine old homes that were

Coffee at Etcetera Café in Lower Town.

John Spurlin and Alan Rhodes welcome visitors to Etcetera in Lower Town.

desecrated into boardinghouses to accommodate the flood of workers needed at the atomic plant have been restored and refurbished. The influx of artists makes Lower Town attractive. The Etcetera Café is "the place to go." The menu features "new" exotic dishes and drinks that quickly get a following. Exhibits are stimulating and changing to maintain the aura of art. The homes in the area sparkle, luring a growing influx of gifted and stimulating inhabitants. Exhibits hanging include works from within the Lower Town area but also traveling exhibits. Even the fire hydrants in this area display wry wit. People greet one another, pedestrians are often leashed to their pets and strangers smile and wave.

Chapter 13

PADUCAH NOBILITY

In an editorial dated May 20, 1979, editor Jack Paxton of the *Paducah Sun-Democrat* reported that the title "Duke of Paducah" had been accorded originally to Irvin Cobb, Paducah's favorite son; however, Benjamin Frances Ford, a well-known country comedian and banjo picker, was the first to use the title professionally. Ford was born in DeSoto, Missouri, and performed with Gene Autry on WLS in Chicago. He also appeared on *Barn Dance*, NBC's *Plantation Party* and, migrating south, became a fixture on the *Grand Ole Opry* in Nashville (where he was inducted into the Country Music Hall of Fame in 1986 after his death). En route, Ford was in St. Louis in 1935 on radio station KWK. Trying for a unique identity, Arnold Roone, a salesman for the station originally from Paducah, suggested that Ford should use the title "Duke of Paducah." Ford did and always appeared in a green hat, green pants, green coat with brass buttons and high-button shoes. His closing line, which became his trademark, was: "I'm goin' to the wagon; these shoes are killin' me!"

Later, according to Paxton, Cobb was visiting at the hotel bearing his name with Fred Neuman, an old friend who wrote one of the better Cobb biographies. Cobb heard Ford's radio program and remarked that Ford's persona was so well known that he brought more recognition to Paducah than Cobb, so Cobb more or less conceded the title to Ford. Neuman sent Ford a crate of strawberries, a crop for which Paducah was famous in the 1940s, and a telegram asking Ford to come to Paducah. He did and became fast friends with Neuman. On arrival at Paducah, Neuman introduced Ford to the locals as follows: "This is the guy that says, 'I'm goin' to the wagon; these shoes are killin' me.'"

Paxton's account of the naming of the Duke of Paducah also told a tale that was later amplified by Christopher Ash in the local newspaper on June 22, 1986. Billie Jacobs, wife of former mayor George Jacobs, remembered that the award developed from a meeting with her husband and "Whitey" Ford at the fair in Metropolis in 1953. Mayor Jacobs told Ford that everywhere he went, people knew of Ford's stage role and insisted on extending the title of "Duke of Paducah" to the mayor. Jacobs got Ford to agree to come to Paducah and receive "official" recognition of his assumed title, hoping to bring publicity to the community. Thus the idea for an official award was born. The first awards were made later that year to Ford and others, including former mayors Robert Cherry, Wayne C. Smith, Pierce E. Lackey and James P. Smith. The first duchess, Miss Lennie W. McLaughlin, was the winner of a beauty contest. The new duchess had to accept a duke's certificate, as the female version, designed by Mrs. Warren Middleton, was not yet ready.

The original Duke of Paducah certificate, designed by Mrs. Elizabeth Hurst Bunchman, a teacher at Jackson School, portrayed a rather foppish gent with a top hat and monocle holding a cigarette. (Later, Mayor Murphy removed the cigarette.) Currently, the seal of the city, replete with the legendary Chief Paduke, adorns the document.

Recipients of the ducal titles range from beauty queens to presidents. Since 1988, a varied mix is evident. Julia Anguelova was a visitor from Bulgaria. Kathrine Peden had been a candidate for governor of Kentucky. Others receiving awards include Margaret and Bill Schraeder, publishers of Paducah; Kala Stroup, president of Murray State University and Southeast Missouri University and head of higher education in that sister state; Albert Gore Jr., then U.S. senator; George Crounse, local shipping magnate and benefactor of education; Craven Crowell, head of TVA; former governor Brereton Jones; Robert Sexton of the Pritchett Committee on education; U.S. representative Joe Kennedy; President George H.W. Bush; and real bluegrass royalty Rick Pitano.

Chapter 14

BARBECUE ON THE RIVER

For nineteen years, from Broadway to Madison and from the floodwall to Fourth, charcoal-stoked ovens and grills have enticed crowds of pedestrians and whet their appetites. Bands and strolling entertainers appear at last light. Smoke from the grills only adds to the wonderful aroma. Unlike many other festivals, proceeds after expenses go to various charities. This event challenges crews of volunteer chefs and servers to serve what is almost a continuous stream of people from early morning to near midnight. Various vocal and instrumental groups are dispersed throughout the area. Streets are closed to vehicular traffic, except in emergencies. Good humor prevails even if one has to walk ten blocks to get access to the barbecue area. Local police have a communication trailer in the area to ensure safety. Tents with chairs and tables are available.

Each contestant takes great care applying the special sauces that give the product its unique flavor. Often, these are treasured family recipes. All through the night, fires burn, embers glow and meat is turned. At daylight, the Barbecue on the River comes alive. Traffic flows toward the delicious aroma. The constant flow of pedestrians eases through the pit areas and scans the displays. Customers consume roasted ears of corn, ribs, shoulder and many newly discovered dishes from the grills, such as that of Marshall Green. Paducah parties hard and long.

Laurel Black described the aura of the festival as one of "friendliness" in a front-page article in the *Paducah Sun* for September 28: "Former circuit cooker Steve Gann says Barbecue on the River offers something that even

The downtown area of Paducah traditionally was the center of entertainment, with theaters and opera houses, among other entertainments. It is not uncommon to see several blocks closed off and used for amusement. Mayor Gerry Montgomery cut into the floodwall to provide a stage downtown that continues to host both local and national acts. Streets are closed for events such as the Summer Festival and Barbecue on the River. The riverfront rocks. A bandstand below the floodwall on Broadway accommodates the Paducah Symphony and other productions. Still, many of the downtown structures are deteriorating or are underutilized. Offices for rail and barge companies, like the Paducah and Louisville and Crounce (river industry), have moved downtown. The chamber of commerce also has relocated.

one of the world's largest pork barbecue competition doesn't." The unique ingredient here is friendliness. "We sit down at the tables and mingle with people," said Gann, a member of the Memphis-based barbecuers the Beasty Boys. Gann pointed out that "they've competed in the World Championship Barbecue Cooking Contest at Memphis in May, one of the largest and most well-known barbecue competitions." In Memphis, contestants are not allowed to connect with the public. In Paducah, participants are allowed to sell food to the public and to "get to know their customers."

The festival ends quietly. Folks get up to attend church the next day. Paducah cleans up.

Chapter 15

MURALS ON THE FLOODWALL

The horrific flood of 1937 nearly destroyed Paducah; however, the resulting floodwall has proved its ability to safeguard residents on more than one occasion since, including the rise in 2011 that brought the river to its highest point since 1937. The presence of a vast wall of blank concrete proved to be a challenge. Muralists with Robert Dafford and Company work with the local preservation committee to supervise the mural panels that now reach over four city blocks. Care is taken to ensure that the subject is important, that the art brings the topic alive and that the result is historically accurate. Bronze plaques before each scene are carefully worded and

Delta Queen at the foot of Broadway, 1980. It is no longer in service.

One of the treasures of downtown Paducah is the collection of murals by Robert Dafford & Co. The Floodwall Mural Advisory Board selects the topics and collects the funds from private doners. The city helps on maintenance and covering the cost of the bronze interpretative panels. From dawn to dusk, one sees both young and old walkers admiring the murals. Passing cars, frequently with out-of-town license plates, creep by. The Floodwall Mural Advisory Board has the final say about what goes on the panels, and an effort is made to ensure that they are both significant and historically accurate. Topics vary from prehistory to current events that have occurred in Paducah, Kentucky, the Atomic City.

Robert Dafford mural commemorating organized labor in Paducah.

Robert Dafford mural featuring the Carson Coca/Cola plant.

Opposite, bottom: The floodwall murals are valued as a teaching tool. Here, on October 21, 2013, the entire first grade of Benton, Kentucky public schools traverses the murals, the ICRR steam locomotive and cars, the riverfront and downtown as a learning experience.

Robert Dafford mural showing the three largest riverboats being welcomed by Paducah ambassadors.

The river industry remains a vital contributor to the economic life of Paducah. This mural on the floodwall illustrates how Paducah industry provides maintainance and repair to towboats and barges. With the opening of the Tombigbee Canal, one can go through the Tennessee River and take the canal to the Gulf of Mexico, a route that is shorter than going down the Mississippi to the Gulf. As a result, Paducah is now a hub. The widening of the Panama canal will allow larger container ships to bring cargo from Asia to the interior of North America via the inland waterway. Paducah is building a crane capable of handling the larger cargo containers. Ships will come from Asia to Paducah, unload and reship smaller units throughout the inland waterway.

Robert Dafford mural showing the freezing of the Ohio River in 1938. The river is almost a mile wide here.

researched. Tourists, including groups arriving on giant riverboats such as the *American Queen*, regularly walk the length of the mural display.

In 2011, floodwaters again menaced Paducah. This time, the floodwall and pumps held the raging Ohio and Tennessee Rivers at bay. On May 6, water reached 58.6 feet and began to seep under the floodgate on Broadway at Water Street. The area outside the floodwall did have severe damage. Fortunately, this section of McCracken County was sparsely populated in 1937, when the Ohio River stood at 60.8 feet on February 2.

Chapter 16

THE ATOMIC AGE ARRIVES

The presence of the atomic plant in McCracken County proved a stimulus to city of Paducah. Population exploded. Economic well-being flourished. The plant also proved to be a threat. The local workforce stretched to absorb the influx. The city reinvented itself. Society shifted; leaders suddenly were not those born and bred in Paducah. As time passed, reports of strange illnesses crept out of the secret cocoon in which the plant resided. Paducahans learned how to live with the Paducah Gaseous Diffusion Plant (PGDP). Countless school children practiced ducking under their desks and tables should a nuclear detonation or leak occur. When individuals in Paducah began to report dire illness that could be related to prolonged exposure to contamination from the PGDP, concerns about the continued desirability of retaining a plant threatened the well-being of the community. One "whistle blower" was Harold D. Hargan from southern Illinois. Dr. Rex Elliot Hall recently published a definitive study of the career of Harold "Hotsy" Hargan in *Callous Disregard: An Inside Story of the Paducah Gaseous Diffusion Plant*. (Hargan's nickname came from a test four months after starting work at Paducah that revealed he had uranium in his urine; plant jargon put it "tea in his pee.") Layers of secrecy began to unfold; assessments of the contamination at PGDP were disturbing and vivid.

Dr. Hall wrote:

> *The PGDP history of nearly 60 years of lies, cover-ups and deceptions, spanning a number of contractors (Union Carbide, Martin Marietta,*

> *Lockheed, USEC, and Bechtel Jacobs) indicts AEC/DOE as the Godfather in this organizational culture. In fact, criminologists have a name for this phenomenon—state-corporate crime (as opposed to individual, corporate or organized crime). The prototypical example was the collusion between NASA and Morton Thiokol leading to the space shuttle* Challenger *disaster. A paper by A. Bruce, P. Becker, entitled "State-Corporate Crime and PGDP," in* Western Criminology Review *examined Paducah and noted that it provided another classic case, with AEC/DOE as initiator and, later, facilitator of organized criminal activities by the contractors.*

The lawsuit against the PGDP went to the federal appeals court in Louisville, Kentucky. Hargan thought he finally would get a chance to face his foe in an impartial setting; however, the frail Hargan was told to be in court early to testify, but the defense took so long with other witnesses that Hargan's weakened body was not up to taking the stand late in the afternoon. The defense strategy won. The plant is due to close shortly. The tailings and residue left behind will last for centuries.

Hotsy died at age seventy-seven. "Unfortunately, the role of a whistleblower is always going to be troublesome. But there are those with something inside—an intolerance for wrong—that does not allow them to watch quietly and do nothing." Hall's description of Hargan is poignant. Let all say, "God bless those who seek truth and are willing to give of themselves to help others."

Chapter 17

PRESUMPTION OF ART

Paducah, Kentucky, is a city of murals. In 1938–39, John Fulton Folinsbee and his son-in-law, Peter G. Cook, painted a pair of six-and-a-half- by ten-and-a-half-foot murals for the new federal building in the city. The artist was recognized at the time as being among the best in the nation. His work here stirred local opposition and conflict over the choice of topics. These murals painted on pressed wooden panels represented pictorially the westward sweep of the frontier originally advocated by the guardians of culture in Paducah. Later, after World War II, Admiral Eugene Paro, a native of Paducah who had rebuilt a derelict submarine, loaded it with the gold reserves of the government of the Philippines as ballast and escaped the occupying Japanese, led a group from Paducah who added a series of paintings to what was then the post office on the lower floor of the federal building. Many historians felt that the presence of the frontier shaped unique institutions found in the United States of America. In 1961, J. Rowland Snyder, director of the design division, Public Buildings Service, gave approval to mount the twelve murals over the mail-access windows in the lower level of the federal building, then used as the post office.

In 1995, Robert Dafford, noted muralist acclaimed for his *trompe l'oeil* technique, started a grand series of huge depictions of the progress of Paducah from the days of the Mound Builders to the present. This work, funded by individuals and institutions in Paducah, occupies the giant floodwall for three city blocks and is a draw for visitors to Paducah. Another mural was added in 2013 commemorating Boy Scout Troop #1, the seventh in the nation.

Chapter 18

LOWER TOWN REVITALIZATION

Historic change is a process that seems to require an initial idea, one or more supporters of that view who are willing to identify with it and encourage its growth and luck. Paducah was fortunate to have these elements in place during the three terms of Mayor William Paxton. An undated pamphlet (circa 2000) entitled *Paducah Artist Relocation Program* lists specific benefits that would be available to artists interested in relocating. Further information was available from Mark Barone, director of the Paducah Artist Relocation Program, or Julie Harmon. Time proved this program worked. Among the benefits supplied by the city or state were low-interest loan programs; health insurance through the Kentucky Arts Council; websites through the Paducah Artist Relocation Program website; marketing and advertising, both locally and nationally; preservation tax incentives of 20 percent made possible by the Tax Reform Act of 1986 in PL 99-514, Internal Revenue Code, Section 47; community incentives; the Paducah Enterprise Zone Authority, November 14, 1986; and state incentives such as the Kentucky Enterprise Zone created in 1982. It worked. Dr. William Renzulli was one of the first to accept. In 2002, he moved to Paducah, restored a large Victorian house and added a studio and gallery. This proved to be the catalyst of a surge of urban renewal

In 2005, the Paducah Artists Relocation Program was recognized by the Rudy Bruner Award for Urban Excellence with a silver award (one of four). The Rudy Bruner Award report notes:

The City intended from the beginning to use the ARP and the Lower Town Neighborhood Plan as a blueprint, or at least as an incubator, for ideas for revitalizing other neighborhoods. [Lower Town has thirty-three blocks.] *Two nearby neighborhoods have been identified as the next target areas, and planning work is already beginning in the Fountain Avenue area and in Upper Town.*

Chapter 19

PADUCAH SCHOOL OF ART AND DESIGN

A division of West Kentucky Community and Technical College, the new Paducah School of Art and Design was launched by the City of Paducah in 2000 "as a means of revitalizing its historical Lower Town neighborhood. This highly successful program has infused over thirty million dollars into the local economy, earning Paducah international recognition as a historic cultural destination and significantly enriching the cultural life of the region." The brochure for the program noted:

> *In August 2008, a collaboration effort between the City, West Kentucky Community & Technical College, and regional interests created Paducah School of Art to serve the region and anchor the Lower Town Arts District through the creation of a world class art school. The school opened in temporary studios in downtown Paducah and immediately exceeded expectations for its growth.*

The school is a diverse "mix of traditional and non-traditional students and studio artists from the community work side by side in the studios, sharing insights, experience and ideas to the mutual benefit of all."

> *In January of 2013, Paducah School of Art expanded into renovated facilities within Madison Hall in Lower Town. This historic structure houses a greatly expanded, state of the art ceramics studio, as well as studios for new programs in jewelry and metals to further serve the community. The*

Welcome to Paducah School of Art and Design.

> *school also changed its name to Paducah School of Art & Design, reflecting an expanded vision for its programming and the art school's absorption of the college's long standing visual communication program* [that had been housed in a metal building initially on the main campus].

Further growth is anticipated:

> *In Spring of 2014, the school will expand again with completion of a 6,700 square foot sculpture facility located on the Madison Hall property. This new building will house fully equipped studios for clay modeling, wood, and metal fabrication, as well as a foundry and support studios for mold making and bronze casting.*

EPILOGUE

Demolition of buildings in the one hundred block of Broadway started while this manuscript was in progress to make way for the convention center in downtown Paducah. This is symptomatic of the dichotomy present in the attitude of Paducahans toward history: should the past be worshipped or should it be celebrated and revered? One attitude would keep something merely because it is aged; the other recognizes that there is a time for each

A relic sign to Finkle's Fair store on lower Kentucky Avenue.

age. The renovation of the old People's Bank building and its conversion into functional office space is a positive application of preservation. The new convention center is a positive example of progress. What is needed is to synthesize the two approaches and revitalize an aging area of the city before it degenerates into irreparable slums. Paducah is making a practical effort to keep its identity as a river city in the age of the automobile. It remains to be seen whether the future population movements parallel Paducah planning. I think they will. I am positive on Paducah.

Over the years, Paducah has been fortunate to house remarkable individuals. Six have been especially worthy of recognition:

CAESAR KASKEL went to Lincoln and got the president to revoke the expulsion of all Jews from Grant's command.

IRWIN S. COBB was a top war correspondent in World War I; excelled in writing short stories; appeared in movies, including *Steamboat Round the Bend*; and was master of ceremonies at the Oscar Awards, presenting a special award to Shirley Temple.

ADMIRAL EUGENE PARO escaped from the Philippines in a hastily refurbished submarine that used all the gold of the Philippine government as ballast. Later, in Okinawa, he was awarded four times. Retiring to Paducah, he inspired local artists to paint murals in the post office of the federal building.

HENRY "SPEEDIE" ATKINS drowned in 1928, was mummified by A.Z. Hamock and became a local legend. Entire classes of elementary students from Paducah and surrounding areas visited Speedie. In 1980, Velma Hamock and Speedie appeared on ABC's *That's Incredible*. The two flew first class to California.

ALBEN BARKLEY, "the Veep," moved to Paducah in 1898. He rose in the Democratic Party, going to Washington in 1912. In 1948, Barkley and Harry Truman upset Thomas Dewey and his running mate. Barkley was the oldest man to be vice president. In 1952, Barkley failed to gain the presidency and returned to the Senate in 1954. At a mock political convention at Washington and Lee University, Barkley proclaimed that he "would rather be a servant in the house of the Lord than to sit in the seats of the mighty." He died of a massive heart attack.

ROBERT H. GRUBBS attended schools in Paducah and took degrees at Florida and Columbia. Grubbs received the 2005 Nobel Prize in Chemistry (along with Richard R. Schrock and Yves Chauvin) for his work in the field of olefin methahesis.

NOTES

Preface

1. Edmund Flagg, *Far West*, Vol. I (New York, 1838), 77.
2. Donald Jackson, ed., *Letters of the Lewis and Clark Expedition with Related Documents, 1783–1854* (Urbana: University of Illinois Press, 1962), 516n.
3. Ibid., 645.

Chapter 1

4. McCracken County, Deed Book A, Paducah, 103 for plat. Robert Fletcher, as agent for William Clark, made the plat on May 26, 1827. See act approved by the General Assembly, January 11, 1830, which authorized the Town of Paducah (correctly spelled). This act specified that the plans of the town be drawn by Jonathan D. Martin, surveyor of McCracken County.
5. See Curtis, *Reports of Decisions of the Supreme Court*; *Porterfield v. Clark* 2 How 76, 40–61; Williams, *Reports of Cases Argued and Decided in the Supreme Court*, 74–125. Kentucky had to recognize Virginia land claims, particularly military warrants. Porterfield argued that the military warrant took precedence over the treasury warrants under both Virginia and Kentucky law. Generally, this would be true, but Clark's earlier claim held in this case.
6. Thompson, "Paducah Historically," 711–12. Original trustees were Robert Fletcher, Thomas J. Flurnoy [*sic*], Francis A. Harrison, Abel Morgan and James P. Smith in the act approved on January 11, 1830.
7. Minutes of the council, June 17, 1833. Members of the board of health included Richard Brownell, Samuel A. Winters and Joseph Merrell. An ordinance dated April 18, 1834, added two doctors to the board: John S. Goulden and W.W.

Lay. The board was asked to examine the riverbank, but apparently it disagreed and refused to act. See called session, June 16, 1834, when a new board was appointed. Dr. Samuel Withers, John Betts, James McPherson and Joseph Beckman proved to be more effective. Smallpox hit Paducah on March 16, 1836. John Wilson and Pearce Jones had the pox. Communicable diseases were a particular hazard to port cities. Cholera arrived at Paducah in 1832, when the steamboat *Freedom* landed with seventeen dead bodies on board. In 1840, there was another outbreak, milder than before; however, in 1851, a crisis developed. Ten died before the epidemic ended. In 1873, a severe outbreak began with the arrival of the *John Kilgore* from New Orleans. Sixty deaths occurred from May to July. Dr. Rueben Saunders of Paducah developed a cure for cholera by injecting belladonna in 1873.

8. Minutes of the council, June 17, 1833. One year later, the council voted to rent the wood lot to the highest bidder (June 16, 1834). For successful leasers, see Council Book No. 2, p. 25, July 7, 1834.
9. Minutes of the council, June 17, 1833.
10. Neuman, *Story of Paducah*, 129. The original edition of this book was published in 1927. Much of the material is solid; however, on occasion, the newspaper training of Mr. Neuman seems to override his historic judgment. Fable and fact are equally presented. The wharf boat came in 1850.
11. Called council meeting, June 20, 1833.
12. The present municipal distribution system faces a decision that will shape its future for many years to come. The plant pumps from the Tennessee and is in need of renovation. Deep wells are being considered rather than depending on either river for input.
13. Original contract authorized by council meeting, July 22, 1833. Work was ordered checked by Charles C. Russell, George Smedley, John Moseley and Bradford Barbee on September 16, 1833. A cover was ordered built on October 7, 1833, by A.W. Taylor. By June 2, 1835, the trustees had to clean the well and expand its size. Misuse of the bucket led to an ordinance on July 11, 1834, providing for fines for free people or lashes for slaves who damaged the bucket.
14. Minutes of the council, December 2, 1833. The house endangered belonged to a trustee, S.A. McPherson. Report on Water Street ordered at a meeting held on June 16, 1834. The report was made on July 8.
15. This engine was rated as a twenty-four-man-power pumper. Commissioners appointed at the council meeting on May 17, 1838.
16. Relief Company Number 2 was chartered on February 25, 1856. See Acts of Kentucky, 1856, Public, 317–18, for Mechanics Fire Company Number 1, Jersey City, Paducah. This company occupied a building at 124 North Fourth Street.
17. Minutes of the council, June 3,1834.
18. Letton is in the minutes of the council, January 13, 1837. Mr. Combs's more interesting collection was reported on May 30, 1837, as was the snake. In passing, it might be noted that it did not take a work of art to attract the attention of the citizens of Paducah. The regular meeting for July 7, 1834, was called off until the next day so that members of the council could attend the trial of Harvey Reaves for murder. Reaves was later executed. See Battle, Perrin and Kniffin, *Kentucky*, II, 98.

19. Minutes of the council, April 7, 1836, April 16. July 15 was the original target date. Also see minutes of the council, August 6, 1836.
20. Allowed at meeting of the council, August 6, 1836.
21. Ordinance passed on May 10, 1837. At the same session, an ordinance prohibited horse galloping in the corporate limits.
22. Minutes of the council, August 24, 1837.
23. Ibid., August 3, 1838. Fuqua could charge 1 percent on each sale. Apparently, Fuqua was not too busy with auctioneering; he also was a member of the first night watch.
24. A local blacksmith was ordered to build grading equipment on June 23, 1837. Part of Broadway was macadamized from the wharf to Second Street, according to Neuman, *Story of Paducah*, 66.
25. The trustees called for brick sidewalks on June 2,1835, repealed this order for Water Street on November 25, 1835, and again decided on brick on May 30, 1837. Water Street ran parallel to First Street from Kentucky to Broadway about fifty feet closer to the river. Prior to 1841, the street was known as Front Street.
26. Neuman, *Story of Paducah*, 66.
27. As early as the meeting held on May 5, 1834, Paducah had set aside $150 for the improvement of the landing and authorized six laborers to accomplish the work. On June 3, 1834, no flat boat, trading boat or raft was allowed to remain at the public landing longer than three hours without paying a fee of $3 in advance to the supervisor. The town also leased ferry rights, beginning on February 15, 1838. Landing fees for other craft was increased from $3 to $5 if such vessels remained docked longer than three hours to free the area for steamboats landing for fuel and supplies.
28. Each community must build a corpus of law that supports and invites businesses to seek protection within that framework. Frequently, special incentives are necessary to nurture new ventures.
29. Minutes of the council, August 16, 1837. Trustees of the bank included C.C. Russell, J.B. Husbands, Eli Houston and Valentine Owen.
30. Denominations issued by the Exchange Bank were 75, 50, 25, $12\frac{1}{2}$ and $6\frac{1}{4}$ cents. Braxton Small was also county clerk when the seat of McCracken County was transferred from Wilmington to Paducah in accordance with an act of the General Assembly dated December10, 1831.Water being high at the time, Small transferred all the county records in a small skiff. Small figured prominently in the city and county. He married Grace Walterson on March 1, 1831, in the first recorded marriage in Paducah. His daughter, Adelaide, was born on December 23, 1831, also a first, according to Neuman, *Story of Paducah*, 103.
31. Battle, Perrin, and Kniffin, *Kentucky*, II, 88.
32. Ibid. Oak Grove became the city cemetery in 1847. Prior to that date, a site on Fourth between Washington and Clark had been used for burials. See Neuman, *Story of Paducah*, 68.
33. Houses numbered according to census taker's book: Nolen (3), Given (7), Hart (11), J. Grief (51), Puryear (40). Also see William F. Norton, merchant, and boarders John Brandon, eighteen, and George B. Grundy, twenty-four, clerks

(74); William J. Dinwiddie, carpenter, and George T. Shanks, twenty-five, and George G. Darro, twenty-two, same (133).

34. Houses are numbered by McCurty as follows: Leonard Roche (83) and Theophilous Roche (82).

35. Battle, Perrin, and Kniffin, *Kentucky*, II, 90–91.

36. Ibid.

37. *Paducah Daily Democrat*, January 3, 1854, 1. Tuition was sixty dollars with board. This issue also lists the faculty of the school located on the northeast corner of Fifth and Kentucky.

38. Battle, Perrin, and Kniffin, *Kentucky*, II, 89. For an early advertisement of the seminary, see *Paducah Daily Democrat*, January 3, 1854, 4. The male academy was located on Contest Road (now Ninth Street) on land donated by John W. Jones. It was not successful.

39. Minutes of the council, August 25, 1843; April 15, 1853.

40. Carlton J. Corliss, *Main Line of Mid-America*, 262–63, quoting a newspaper account. John Lawson was the engineer on this first run. In his later years, Lawson claimed to have been the engineer of the first successful railroad in his native England in 1827. See biographical sketch in the *Paducah News–Democrat*, November 20, 1901. This article quotes an interview with the ninety-six-year-old Lawson, who was living in St. Louis at the time. Ironically, the article came out the week Lawson died. See *Paducah News-Democrat*, November 28, 1901, 9, for obituary.

Lawson claimed to have worked for George Stephenson on the Manchester–Liverpool railroad. Lawson came to the United States with an engine, which he named the Herald after the ship that brought Lawson and the engine from England. Lawson ran the engine on a ten-mile line from Baltimore to Green Springs in 1829, as per his agreement with Stephenson.

Lawson's claim is contrary to most generally accepted histories of railroads, which give the honor of operating the first successful railroad trip to George Stephenson in 1829. See *Memorial Record of Western Kentucky*, I, 288–90; Neuman, *Story of Paducah*, 41–42, 107, 255. In the former, it is claimed that Wilson "built" the first locomotive used by Stephenson and the one he accompanied to America. Later, he worked for the Baldwin Locomotive Works in Philadelphia before coming to Paducah in 1840. Lawson turned to the river in later years. He joined the Confederacy, supervising the construction of a steam ram at Yazoo. After the fall of Vicksburg, Lawson joined the army as an elderly private in the Third Kentucky Cavalry.

Lawson remained active and alert until his death. He served as the "engineer" of the federal building in Paducah during the first administration of Grover Cleveland. Lawson's house was at the northeast corner of Seventh and Broadway.

CHAPTER 2

41. Hamilton, "Kentucky's Linn Boyd," 185–95. Note that Linn Boyd was a Democrat, while Clay was a Whig. Boyd moved to Paducah from Trigg County. See *Biographical Directory of the American Congress*, 853. Boyd was made Speaker of

the House on December 5, 1851, and served until 1854. He was elected lieutenant governor of Kentucky in 1859 but died on December 17. Boyd County was created in 1860 and named for Linn Boyd.

42. Among the earliest settlers were Morris and Abraham Uri and Leopold Klaw—all Jews. The founders of the burial society included A. Goldsmith, Jacob Weil, L. Harris, M. Lieber, J. Bodenheimer, Daniel Wolf and others. Issac Bernheim, in *Settlement of Jews*, cites the Shane, Alexander and Friedlander families as being in Paducah in 1863. Other early Jews identified by Bernheim are Benjamin Weille, Samuel Dreyfuss, M. Livingston, Leopold Levy, Samuel Rosenfield, Isaac and Jacob Eckstein and Samuel Rexinger. See *Settlement of Jews*, 21, 22, 78. Bernheim moved to Louisville and founded the distilleries there.

43. Battle, Perrin, and Kniffin, *Kentucky*, II, 91–94.

44. Shannon and McQuown, *Presidential Politics*, passim, 6–38. The *Louisville Journal*, November 27, 1861, 3, gives the returns; however, the eight votes for Lincoln are omitted.

CHAPTER 3

45. Battle, Perrin, and Kniffin, *Kentucky*, II, 81. Also see minutes of the council, April 19, 1861 (Order Book Six, 51).

46. Collins, *History of Kentucky*, I, 87–88; Stickles, *Simon Bolivar Buckner*, 55; Moore, *Rebellion Record*, I, 72–76.

47. *War of the Rebellion*, Series I, Vol. III, Part 2, 67, 89; hereafter cited as *OR*. Also see *Military History of Kentucky*, 162.

48. McElroy, *Kentucky in the Nation's History*, 532–33, quoting a letter from the Buckner MSS; also see *Nashville Republican Banner*, June 18, 1861, quoted in Stickles, *Simon Bolivar Buckner*, 71.

49. Battle, Perrin, and Kniffin, *Kentucky*, I, 358. Buckner had known Pillow during the Mexican War. There was bad feeling between them.

50. Stickles, *Simon Bolivar Buckner*, 61; *Louisville Daily Courier*, June 15, 1861, l.

51. S.B. Bickner to W.P. Mellon, June 25, 1861, in Magoffin Papers, quoted in Stickles, *Simon Bolivar Buckner*, 71.

52. Johnson and Cassiday to Buckner, Magoffin Papers, quoted in Stickles, *Simon Bolivar Buckner*, 71.

53. *Report of the Adjutant General*, 84; Thompson, *History of the Orphan Brigade*, 44.

54. Such meetings were not uncommon on the Louisville and Nashville Railroad line. No violence resulted. Each side was willing to postpone creating an issue in neutral Kentucky—for a while longer.

55. Frémont's understanding of the situation was based on poorly organized and imperfectly screened intelligence reports that indicated an ominous buildup of Confederate forces in southeastern Missouri. General William J. Hardee was thought to be planning an imminent attack on Ironton. Another large force was thought to be near Benton, some eighteen miles south and ten miles inland from

Cape Girardeau. A smaller contingent of Confederates was at Commerce, fifteen miles south of the river—all under the command of General Pillow.

Grant was ordered to defend Cape Girardeau. Colonel W.H.L. Wallace from Bird's Point, just across the river from Cairo, and Benjamin M. Prentiss from Ironton were to reinforce Grant. Troops from Cairo were to reconnoiter at the river near Belmont, just opposite Columbus.

After driving the Confederates out of Missouri, Grant was to move into Kentucky, take Columbus and develop an offensive into Southern territory. Grant would have to break the neutrality of Kentucky to execute his orders. Ordinarily, departmental commanders do not have the prerogative to change the policy of presidents, but rapid developments in the local theater and a lack of communication between Frémont and Washington allowed him to commit the nation to a matter of military expedience. As it was, Polk beat Frémont to Columbus. The Confederate position was not as Frémont thought. Hardee was withdrawing into Arkansas. Pillow had pulled back to New Madrid and was erecting the defensive works, not planning to attack. Grant did make the reconnaissance to Belmont. This, plus events at Paducah, prompted Polk to take Hickman and Columbus and put Kentucky into the war.

56. *OR*, Series I, IV, 178. There were three gunboats under the command of Commander John Rogers involved in this incident, the *Lexington*, the *Tyler* and the *Conestoga*. Hereafter Series I will be assumed in *OR* unless otherwise cited.
57. Ibid., 176–77.
58. Collins, *History of Kentucky*, I, 93.
59. *OR*, IV, 177; Oglesby to Frémont.
60. Ibid., 179
61. Ibid., 180. J.G. Deupree described the Confederate advance in "Noxubee Squadron," 22, as follows: "Early in September, the cavalry were ferried across the river and rode to Hickman, Kentucky, whither General [Frank] Cheatham and a brigade of infantry had gone on a steamboat. Dense columns of smoke were visible far up the river. Women and children were screaming in the streets, as we arrived; bugles were sounded; and guns were placed in commanding positions to resist an expected attack, for a large force was believed to be coming down, threatening the capture of Hickman." Union gunboats were scouting to see what was happening; nevertheless, the population welcomed the Rebels as saviors. Pillow's field artillery turned back the boats without loss to either side.
62. Grant, *Personal Memoirs*, I, 264–65.
63. *OR*, IV, 196–97.
64. Grant, *Personal Memoirs*, I, 158.
65. Ibid.
66. Ibid
67. See proclamation, p. 30.
68. Ibid. The site for the marine hospital had been jointly deeded to the Federal government by William Clark and Robert Porterfield, pending the outcome of the litigation between them. After the Supreme Court acted, the deed was tendered and the hospital built in 1849–51. See Battle, Perrin and Kniffin, *Kentucky*, II, 94, for a description of the building. Fire destroyed the hospital in

1862 while it was being used to store ammunition. For deed, see Deed Book A, p. 96, recorded on December 25, 1845.

69. *OR*, II, 166: "I regret to inform you that Confederate forces inconsiderable number have invaded the territory of Kentucky and are occupying and fortifying the strong positions at Hickman and Chalk Bluffs." The Chalk Bluffs are just below Columbus. Also see *OR*, II, 471, and Grant, *Personal Memoirs*, I, 159. For Grant's report, see *OR*, IV, 197.
70. *OR*, IV, 180.
71. Ibid., 181.
72. Ibid., 189.
73. Ibid., 190.
74. Ibid., 185.
75. Ibid., 185–87.
76. October 8, 1862, in Collins, *History of Kentucky*, I,96. A sudden rise of the river from twelve to thirteen feet broke up the bridge. It was not rebuilt.
77. *OR*, III, 528, Grant to Captain Chauncey McKeever, October 9. For an excellent survey of the entire period, see Catton, *Grant Moves South*.
78. *OR*, III, 167–68, Colonel Wagner to Grant.
79. Battle, Perrin, and Kniffin, *Kentucky*, I, 165.
80. *OR*, III, 167.
81. Ibid.
82. Ibid., 168–69.
83. Ibid., 487, Grant to Oglesby and Waagner, September 11.
84. Ibid.
85. The Federals were defeated at Lexington by Sterling Price. Frémont's instructions to Grant are in *OR*, III, 489. Also see Johnson and Buell, *Battles and Leaders*, 307–13.
86. *OR*, III, 501–02.
87. Ibid., 511.
88. Report from W.H.L. Wallace at Bird's Point, 2:00 a.m.
89. *OR*, III, 268.
90. Ibid., 269. Oglesby was sent new orders on the fifth to swing south toward New Madrid and, when he passed the road leading to Belmont, to contact Grant there. Colonel Wallace was to join Oglesby from Bird's Point.
91. General O.F. Smith, in a letter to Adjutant General Townsend on November 6, gave this estimate of the Confederate strength: "At Columbus and vicinity there are 10,000 men; on the opposite shore 2,000; near Mayfield 2,500; at Memphis 3,000; and at Bowling Green 40,000. The enemy can concentrate at Columbus at any time 30,000 men." See Battle, Perrin, and Kniffin, *Kentucky*, I, 380. For actual count, see *OR*, III, 730; there were 16,307 actually at Columbus.
92. Grant, *Personal Memoirs*, I, 269, 271–72.
93. Ibid., I, 164–67.
94. *OR*, III, 299–300.
95. City officials consulted with the military concerning the elections held in the summer of 1862. This was to comply with the order of General Jeremiah T.

Boyle, who became commander of the Department of Kentucky in June 1862. Boyle issued orders requiring only loyal citizens to run for office. See letter of Mayor John Sauner to John R. Howett, provost marshal, July 29, 1862, in minutes of the council, Order Book Six, 118–19.

As a general rule, the German population in the Ohio Valley supported the cause of the Union. Jakob Oehlschlaeger entered the Union army and became the personal bodyguard of General W.T. Sherman. This is attested to by his discharge, currently in the possession of John Oehlschlaeger. Among the German Jews, Samuel Rexinger was listed as a private and rose to the rank of captain. Emmanuel Fels went into the Confederate service and spent four years of honorable service there. See Bernhein, *Settlement of Jews*, 22, 78.

96. Catton, *Grant Moves South*, 87.

97. Ibid., quoting Smith Papers and a letter of John P. Hawkins, a staff officer of Halleck's, writing in 1906 in *Reunion Book*, 92–93; "Recollections of the Fallen," *Army and Navy Journal*, July 8, 1865. When Tilghman joined the Confederacy, his wife, Augusta, and two sons caught the last boat south to Clarksville, Tennessee.

98. *OR*, VII, 122–23, Foote's report; VII, 140, Tilghman's report. Also see Jesse Taylor, "The Defense of Fort Henry," in *Battles and Leaders*, I, 370. In high water, the fort was rendered useless. Tilghman surrendered with his token force after his cannons were either flooded or destroyed by the fire of the gunboats.

99. The Confederates abandoned Columbus on February 27; the Federals entered and took possession of the "Gibralter of the West" on March 3. See Collins, *History of Kentucky*, I, 101.

100. Ibid. Also see Battle, Perrin, and Kniffin, *Kentucky*, II, 89. The same spire had been destroyed by a tornado on August 9, 1851, along with two boats and a hotel (the Marshall House, later called the Richmond House). The *Dover* and the *Caledonia* were sunk. Six other boats were severely damaged.

101. Battle, Perrin, and Kniffin, *Kentucky*, II, 89.

102. Collins, *History of Kentucky*, I, 124. Federal officials claimed that some merchants had more on hand than they had sold the previous two years. In effect, they had become the commissary of the Confederacy.

103. Ibid., I, LXIII, Part 2, 860; III, V, 103–05.

CHAPTER 4

104. *OR*, XVII, Part 2, 424. Also see Korn, *American Jewry*, 122.

105. Korn, *American Jewry*, 124. Wolff was a leader of the Jewish community in Paducah and is styled as being a "rabbi" by one source. See Battle, Perrin, and Kniffin, *Kentucky*, II, 93.

106. *OR*, XVII, Part 2, 530, 540; XIV, Part 1, 9.

107. Preserved in a play, *Highlights of Paducah Jewish History*, by Mrs. Max Kaufman and Mrs. Ted Rosenberg, performed at Temple Israel in 1955. Copy in the Temple files.

108. Collins, *History of Kentucky*, I, 104–05.

109. Ibid. The vote was quite light. Union ticket supporters won everywhere because the military controlled the polls. For compliance in Paducah, see minutes of the council, July 29–30, 1862, in Order Book Six, 118–19.
110. Collins, *History of Kentucky*, I, 106.
111. Ibid.
112. Ibid.
113. Ibid., 107.
114. Ibid.
115. Ibid.
116. As early as September 1861, the Senate had passed a measure setting severe penalties on any Kentuckian who joined military forces that later invaded the state; however, the House refused to concur. On October 1, virtually the same law was enacted declaring native Kentuckians invading the state to be judged guilty of a felony. Enlistment in the Confederacy was a misdemeanor punishable by a fine of not more than $1,000 or imprisonment of not more than six months. See Acts of Kentucky, 1861, 15.

Additional reinforcement of civil penalties came in December; and in the session of March 1862, the legislature passed the expatriation law that provided that any citizen who joined the Confederate government, either in a civil or military capacity, or who should give voluntary aid or assistance to those in opposition to the Federal government, shall be "deemed to have expatriated himself, and shall no longer be a citizen of Kentucky, nor shall he again be a citizen except by permission of the legislature." See Acts of Kentucky, 1862, 71. Each session of the legislature seemed to increase the volume of laws designed to punish Confederates and their followers.
117. *OR*, Series III, IV, 138. Prior to the visit ofthe adjutant general, most blacks enrolled in the military had been in noncombat duties.
118. Franklin, *From Slavery to Freedom*, 232.The death rate of the colored regiment at Paducah was over twice that of most white units, perhaps due to exposure to communicable diseases for the first time. For numbers, see the appendix of *Report of the Adjutant General*, II, 43–149.The following is a report of the Eighth Heavy Artillery, Colored:

Co.	# Listed	Died	KIA	Disch.	Transf.	Desert.
A	110	37	0	16	19	11
B	114	36	0	11	1	6
C	91	46	2	15	5	12
D	58	46	0	0	0	4
E	89	46	0	8	36	17
F	86	31	0	10	0	26
G	91	31	0	16	1	11
H	102	42	0	10	0	11
I	103	41	0	4	0	7
K	91	50	0	11	0	3
L	58	27	0	9	0	30

The Emancipation Proclamation of January 1, 1863, freed slaves only in Rebel territory occupied by Federal forces; thus, it did not apply to Kentucky. Slavery was legal in Kentucky after the Civil War ended. Passage of the Thirteenth Amendment to the Constitution and its proclamation on December 18, 1865, finally freed Kentucky slaves.

The presence of black soldiers in Paducah was a source of displeasure to the population and also served as a challenge to the Confederates. The latter felt that some example must be made to discourage the practice. This seems to have been one motive behind the raids of Nathan Bedford Forrest in 1864. For a good study of the Negro in the Civil War, see Benjamin Quarles, *The Negro in the Civil War* (Boston, 1953) and Dudley T. Cornish, *The Sable Arm: Negro Troops in the Union Army, 1862–1865* (New York, 1956).

119. Collins, *History of Kentucky*, I, 132.
120. Battle, Perrin, and Kniffin, *Kentucky*, II, 84; *Report of the Adjutant General*, II, 338.
121. George, *History of the 3rd, 7th, 8th and 12th Kentucky*; *Military History of Kentucky*, 207; Collins, *History of Kentucky*, I, 132–33.
122. George, *History of the 3rd, 7th, 8th and 12th Kentucky*, 76.
123. Ibid., 77. Thompson was killed near his own house.
124. *Military History of Kentucky*, 207; Collins, *History of Kentucky*, I, 133.
125. George, *History of the 3rd, 7th, 8th and 12th Kentucky*.
126. Major Barnes of the Sixteenth Kentucky Cavalry burned the houses near the fort.
127. Sandburg, *Abraham Lincoln*, 421.
128. George, *History of the 3rd, 7th, 8th and 12th Kentucky*, 78.
129. Ibid. Note that George says that 150 men took part in the demonstration at Columbus while J. Clay Horne, commanding part of the detachment, says 110. See *Columbus Dispatch*, October 31, 1867, responding to a letter in the *Louisville Courier* of October 16, which quoted the *New York Times* of September 25, 1867.
130. H.T. Reid to Grant, February 18, 1864, in *OR*, XXXII, Part 2, 427.
131. Ibid., Part 1, 512.
132. Ibid., Part 3, 233.
133. Ibid., Part 1, 515; XLI, Part 2, 535.
134. Ibid., XXXIX, Part 2, 171, July 11.
135. Collins, *History of Kentucky*, I, 134.
136. Ibid., 135.
137. Ibid., 136.
138. *OR*, XXXIX, Part 2, 144; Kerr, *History of Kentucky*, II, 879–80; *Senate Journals*, 1865, 26–27, for report to Kentucky legislature by a special committee sent to Paducah to investigate.
139. *Senate Journal*, 1865, 26.
140. Collins, *History of Kentucky*, I, 138.
141. *Senate Journals*, 1865, 26–27.
142. *Military History of Kentucky*, 211.
143. Collins, *History of Kentucky*, I, 138. At the same time, Paine also banished a group from Columbus that included Mrs. Dowell, Mr. Malone, James Moore,

McKean Hubbard, Judge Vance, N. Cooke, George B. Moore, Pembroke Walker, Burns Walker, James Morton and R.E. Cooke.

For a sympathetic view of Paine, see the letter of A.L. Hunt to his mother on August 14,1864, from Headquarters District of West Kentucky at Paducah in A.L. Hunt Papers, Southern Historical Collection, Library, University of North Carolina–Chapel Hill. Hunt reported the eviction of Mrs. Wollfolk [*sic*] under Negro guard to Canada. The trip cost $350, but the money came from the Rebels. "The General levies a tax of $125.00 on every bale of cotton and 25% per hundred on every hogshead of tobacco that comes into the city—owned by the rebs—on persons of doubtful loyalty—to form a fund for repaying union families that live in the neighborhood who have had their houses burned by the guerrillas. He paid a union woman—whose husband had been hung by the rebs for adhering to his union sentiments—a thousand dollars of this fund—he would pay her a thousand more. That's the right kind of doctrine."

144. *Paducah Daily News*, February 5, 1883, 1. John G. Fisher, a German, was mayor during the Paine era.

145. Collins, *History of Kentucky*, I, 140. General Stephen Burbridge was a radical Republican and did not hesitate to use his position as the military commander of Kentucky to further the cause of his party. Anyone espousing the cause of the Democratic Party was suspect. Even the loyal *Lexington Observer* had its paper supply cut off for support of McClellan in 1864.

On October 26, Burbridge published General Order No. 8, which provided that "hereafter, no guerrilla will be received as prisoners; and any officer who may capture such, and extend to them the courtesies due to prisoners of war, will be held accountable for disobedience of orders." This act did not end guerrilla raids. In fact, the bulk of western Kentucky was controlled by irregulars until the end of the war. Even the Confederates had to take action against the irregulars. See the letter of Forrest from West Point, Mississippi, March 18, 1865, in Kerr, *History of Kentucky*, II, 904–05.

146. Collins, *History of Kentucky*, I, 140–41; see Governor Bramlette's message in *Senate and House Journal*, 1865, for particulars of charges.

147. Meredith took command on September 8. See *OR*, XXXIX, Part 3, 155; Collins, *History of Kentucky*, I, 141.

148. Collins, *History of Kentucky*, I, 151–55; *Senate Journals*, 1865, 11. General Paine was court-martialed but acquitted. Joseph Holt of Kentucky was the advocate general at the time and is accused of omitting some of the more damaging charges against Paine in the trial. See Collins, *History of Kentucky*, I, 157; however, this view might be biased.

Guerrillas continued to operate in and near Paducah until the end of the war. On March 29, a Captain McDougall led a Rebel band against Captain Gregory—both were killed. This action was memorialized in a poem that appeared in the *Federal Union*, April 7, 1865, 4. The poem by Mattie J. Bradley was to be sung to the tune of "Spare the Old Homestead." For the attitude of Paducahans upon learning that peace had returned, see Order Book Six, April 17, 1865, 315.

CHAPTER 5

149. Freedmen's Affairs in Kentucky and Tennessee gives regular reports on the activities of the bureau. Judge Wiley P. Fowler of the Paducah Circuit declared the Freedman's Bureau law unconstitutional. See Grubbs, *4 Keys to Kentucky*, 121. Nothing came of Fowler's ruling.
150. Clark, *History of Kentucky*, 200–01; *Paducah Sun–Democrat*, Centennial Edition, August 1, 1956, Section B–4, article on the First Baptist Church by Don Pepper.
151. *Paducah Daily News*, January 21, 1875, 4. In the February 13, 1886, issue of this paper, there is a report of a Negro who tried to run for city council, only to be beaten—physically.
152. *News-Democrat*, November 5, 6,7, 1901, l. The Republican, Augustus Wilson, won the governor's race as well.
153. *News-Democrat*, July 16, 1911, l.
154. Ibid., July 26, 1911, l.
155. Ibid., August 9, 1911, l. The Illinois Central ran six special excursion trains into Paducah to accommodate the crowd.
156. *News-Democrat*, August 19, 1911, l.
157. Ibid., November 8, 1911, l.
158. Ibid., November 9, 1911, l. Police and firemen were rotated by the party in power. Employees in the Street Department also were political appointees. Hazelip offended many by appointing blacks to city posts to repay political debts.
159. *News-Democrat*, March 1913, passim, April 1, 1913, l.
160. Ibid., April 8, 1913, 1. The office of the paper was flooded, but the paper used the equipment of Young Printing on the second floor to put out a reduced-sized issued during the worst part of the flood.
161. *News-Democrat*, November 5, 1913, l.
162. *Burns v. Lackey*.
163. Ibid., deposition of Burns et al., 7.
164. Ibid., deposition of the plaintiff, 6–7 for copy of constitution of the Independent Club. Founders of the club included George Jacobs, Henley Franklin, George Hannin, E.H. Pell, John C. Hast, F.S. Johnson and Thomas Culver.
165. *News-Democrat*, May 16, 1916, 2 for *Birth of a Nation*. The Elks minstrel reported on January 13, 1916, 8; and January 16, 1916, 5.
166. Ibid., January 18, 1916, l.
167. Ibid., November 2, 1915, l.
168. Ibid., January 29, 1916, l.
169. Ibid., February 27, March 1, 1916, l. The secretary of the February meeting was Van Davis, a Negro.
170. Kentucky Reports, Vol. 171, 1916, 21; *Burns v. Lackey*. Hazelip was also charged with being "an intense Republican."
171. *News-Democrat*, June 23, 1916, l.
172. Ibid., June 25, 1916, l.
173. Ibid., October 21, 1916, l. Note that Wallace, who led the field in 1915, did not run at all. He had won among the people and with the governor but could not cope with the court-mandated third race.

174. *Paducah Evening Sun*, October 24, 1916, 1. This claimed to be Republican in national politics and independent in local issues.
175. *Paducah Evening Sun*, November 6, 1916, 1.
176. Ibid., November 8, 1916, 1. Ten full-time and two part-time police were fired. See issue of November 28, 1916, 1. Hazelip's discomfiture was temporary. He was elected to the commission again in the November 1917 elections; his "People's Ticket" split city posts with the Municipal Ownership faction headed by W.A. Gardner.
177. *News-Democrat*, September 3, 1918, 1; October 15, 1918, 1.
178. Ibid., September 8, 1918, 1; October 19, 1918, 1.
179. Ibid., passim, September 1918.
180. Ibid. Conroy died on September 28; Charles enlisted on October 6. See p. 1.
181. Ibid., September 15, 1918, 1.
182. Ibid., October 8, 1918, 1, for closing of public places; on October 11, five hundred new cases of flu were reported; no meeting of any kind was allowed by October 13; saloons were to close early on October 19; the death toll was announced on the front page on October 23–30; and the Kaiser abdicated on November 9, the same day that the "lid" was taken off on the flu epidemic.
183. Ibid., October 21, 1918, 1.
184. Ibid., October 12, 1919, 1. Also see Felix Holt's articleon "the Ferns," November 2, 1919, 1.
185. Ibid., October 15, 1919, 1.
186. Ibid.
187. Ibid., October 19, 1919, 1.
188. Ibid., October 31, 1919, 1.
189. Ibid., November 4, 1919, 1.
190. Ibid., November 5, 1919, 1.
191. Ibid., September 1, 1922, 1.
192. Ibid., September 22, 1922, 1. Former mayor Hazelip was appointed to the federal post on February 7, 1922. He remained in Louisville and died there on November 12, 1950. See Neuman, *Story of Paducah*, 89.
193. *News-Democrat*, November 8, 1922, pl.
194. Ibid., November 2, 1923, 1; November 3, 1923, 1. Some thought Tully would gain votes by his attack on the Klan; he did not. See November 6, 1923, 1. Tully was a candidate for mayor at the time.
195. *News-Democrat*, November 7, 1923, 1. Mrs. Kinsolving lost by 3,307 to 2,525. See November 8, 1923, 2.
196. *News-Democrat*, November 7, 8, 1922, 1. During the furor over the hotly contested election in the city, few took note of an item that appeared in the local papers. Adolf Hitler seized power temporarily in Bavaria in a putsch—an omen of what was to come.
197. *News-Democrat*, November 5, 1924, 1–2. J.G. Fleming won the Sixth Ward contest over Henry Bougeno.
198. *News-Democrat*, November 3, 1926, 1.
199. Ibid., September 2, 1927, 1. Richard Rudy, Con W. Craig, Charles G. Vahlkamp, W.F. Bradshaw and Harry L. Meyer had formed the Ohio River Bridge Company to construct the bridge.

200. *News-Democrat*, November 9, 1927, 1.
201. *Paducah Evening Sun*, November 7, 1928, 1. Smith carried the county by twenty-two votes.
202. *News-Democrat*, November 4, 1931, 1; also see *Paducah Evening Sun*, November 6, 1931, 1.
203. *Paducah Evening Sun*, November 8, 1935, 1.
204. Goodman Papers, Box 4, first folder, September 1–15, 1935.
205. Ibid., February 20–March 28, 1936.
206. Ibid., April–May.
207. Ibid., May–June.
208. Ibid., June–July.
209. Ibid., September 1–15.
210. Ibid.
211. Ibid., December 16–31, 1935.

CHAPTER 6

212. *Paducah Sun-Democrat*, "Disasters," Centennial Edition, July 26, 1956, C-5.
213. Ibid., C-10
214. Ibid., C-3, C-7.
215. Mrs. T.J. Marshall to Tom and Lenore Marshall, Wickliffe, Kentucky, February 4–5, 1937, typescript copy of original in possession of Mrs. Tom Marshall of Paducah.
216. *Paducah Sun-Democrat*, January 3, 1937, 1. On January 7, the same paper noted that Paducah needed to put up matching funds to keep the WPA programs for the coming year. In 1936, five hundred worked on WPA projects in the Paducah area. Still, times looked better. On January 17, an upturn in building was reported for the city.
217. Marshall letter.
218. Ibid.
219. Power was restored to 95 percent on January 15. See *Paducah Sun-Democrat*, January 15, 1937, 1. The weather bureau predicted a crest of forty-six to forty-seven feet. It rained an inch and a half the next day.
220. Mrs. T.J. Marshall to Tom and Lenore Marshall, Wickliffe, Kentucky, February 4–5, 1937, typescript copy of original in possession of Mrs. Tom Marshall of Paducah.
221. Pell, *Descendants of William Pell*, 147.
222. Ibid.
223. Bill Powell, "The Story of a City and a River," *Paducah Sun-Democrat*, July 26, 1956, C-3.
224. Interview with the author, February 6, 1980. Mayfield was not inhospitable; it was full.
225. O.K. Vick, interview with author, February 22, 1980. Vick was one of the senior Scouts involved in the Lone Oak area.
226. Vick interview. The Scouts got blankets for the refugees later by going to the Cobb Hotel and appropriating all available bed linen.

227. Vick interview. Also see *Paducah Sun-Democrat*, February 14, 1937, 3.

228. *Paducah Sun-Democrat*, February 1937, 1. Three homes on "C" Street were destroyed on the previous day. On the eighteenth, a fire started in the home of Lexton Downey on Park Avenue and spread to that of Gus Hank and two others. See issue for February 2, l.

229. *Paducah Sun-Democrat*, February 12, 1937, l.

230. Ibid.

231. Captain Peterson's efforts were recognized in a citation reported on page 9 of the March 23 issue of the *Paducah Sun-Democrat.* For controversy between Bean and Washburn, see the issues for February 1, 1, and February 10, 1.

232. *Paducah Sun-Democrat*, February 11, 1937, 1; February 13, 1937, 1; February 16, 1937, 1. Hopkins visited Paducah on February 3. Barkley helped arrange for $20 million in 3 percent loans.

Roy Wilkins visited the Ohio Valley and was surprised at the lack of racial discrimination in Louisville; however, at Paducah, two colored doctors, G.A. Davis and P.M. Fernandez, worked day and night, and the Red Cross made no provision for food and shelter other then refugee tickets. White physicians got preferential treatment. See "Through the 1937 Flood Area," *Crisis* 44 (1937): 104–06, 124–26.

233. *Paducah Sun-Democrat*, February 12, 1937, 4. The canteen had opened on January 23.

234. *Paducah Sun-Democrat*, February 18, 1937, l. Four days earlier, damage was estimated at $26,728,000.

235. *Paducah Sun-Democrat*, February 19, 20, 1937, l.

236. Ibid., February 16, 1937, l.

237. Ibid., March 24, 1937, l. Both women were over sixty years of age. The sisters lived in a two-room house and were discovered when the weather warmed.

238. *Paducah Sun-Democrat*, February 19, 1937, l. Five days earlier, Captain Miles Reber of the U.S. Corps of Engineers had met with city officials to explore the feasibility of a floodwall. No one wanted to see towboats moving along Murrell Boulevard or Fountain Avenue again.

239. *Paducah Sun-Democrat*, February 22, 1937, 1.

240. Ibid., March 3, 1937, l. Emmett Durrett was chairman of the Workers Alliance; O.A. Kerth, was treasurer; Madge Reeves, secretary; and W.E. Barnes signed as organizer of the Paducah branch.

241. Fred Neuman, "Sidelights on Paducah," a regular feature column, *Paducah Sun-Democrat*, March 23, 1937.

CHAPTER 7

242. *Paducah Sun-Democrat*, November7, 8, 9, 1939. 1. Lackey got 4,934 to 2,662 for Hank.

243. *Paducah Sun-Democrat*, October 14, 17, November 2, 3, 1943, 1.

244. Ibid., November 5, 1947, l.
245. Ibid., November 2, 6, 7, 1951, l.
246. Ibid., November 6, 1955, l.
247. Ibid., November 1, 3, 4, 5, 1956, 1; Robert Cherry, interview with the author, March 6,1980, on audio tape at PCC library; James Munal, interview with the author, March 22, 1980. A recount at the time it was demanded would have compromised the vote of the precinct.
248. *Paducah Sun-Democrat*, November 2, 1963, 1.
249. Ibid., November 5, 1867, l. W.G. Harvey, a black minister, ran fifth. Upon the death of Fellers, Cherry appointed Harvey to fill the term until an election could select a replacement. Thus, Harvey became the first black commissioner. Robert Cherry, interview with the author, March 6, 1980. Harvey defeated James Lynn in the special election to keep his seat on the board.
250. *Paducah Sun-Democrat*, November 3, 1971, 1; W.G. Harvey, interview with the author, March 22, 1980.
251. *Paducah Sun-Democrat*, November 4, 5, 1975, 1. Murphy devoted his entire attention to filling the office of mayor during his term, as he had pledged.
252. *Paducah Sun-Democrat*, November 7, 1979, 1, 10. Three former commissioners were among the losers in the race: Henry Puryear, who had served seven consecutive terms; William Murphy; and William L. Kressenberg. C.R. "Buck" Jones lost his first attempt at the board. Cherry remarked after his defeat, "I won't be back." See interview with Bill Bartleman.

CHAPTER 8

253. Battle, Perrin and Kniffin, *Kentucky*, II, 96; Neuman, *Story of Paducah*, 130–31. For contract, see minutes of the council, August 25, 1843. A new contract was negotiated on April 15, 1853. In the interval, the city threatened to sell the property at auction to force Lovejoy to comply with the contract.
254. Minutes of the council, June 17, 1833.
255. *Paducah Sun-Democrat*, July 25, 1956, B-3.
256. *South Central Bell Telephone Directory*, November 1979, 274.
257. *Cairo (Illinois) Delta*, April 26, 1849, 2, visit to Paducah by editor.
258. Ibid., May 3,1849, 1, quoting the *Paducah Kentuckian*.
259. *News-Democrat*, November 5, 1905; Neuman, *Story of Paducah*, 100.
260. Battle, Perrin and Kniffin, *Kentucky*, II, 96; Deed Book T, 566, April 1, 1870.
261. *Paducah Daily News*, December 17, 1894, 4; *Paducah Daily Register*, August 18,1907, l.
262. *Paducah Daily News*, April 28, 1897, 3. The State of Tennessee wanted to keep the large log for exhibition. For fire, see the *Paducah Evening Sun*, September 27,1906, 2. Even thirty hours of rain did not save the structure. For new location, see the *Paducah Daily Register*, June 25, 1907, l.
263. *Paducah Evening Sun*, September 27, 1906, 2; June 1, 1908, 1; July 23, 1909, l.
264. *Paducah News*, January 5, 1901, 1; January 26, 1901, l.

265. Worthy Manufacturing Company came to Paducah at the instigation of the board of trade (which had succeeded the Commerce Club). Leo F. Keiler asked the management of this Chicago-based company if it would come to Paducah if the city provided a building, as it had done for the International Shoe Company in 1919. The firm was interested; however, no suitable building was available. The board started a script-stamp plan to raise funds to build a structure. Local donations ranging from $1 to $20 raised $75,000, and the building was completed in 1932. Worthy came to Paducah and went broke three years later. Isadore Fine of M. Fine and Company took over, but increased wages doomed this firm, too. Other plants locating in Paducah between 1900 and 1940 include Southern Textile Company, Claussner Hosiery, Priester Hosiery and Cohankus Manufacturing (maker of mops). Southern and Claussner's were Paducah-based organizations, the former based on an invention by E.G. Davis of Paducah. See the *Paducah Sun-Democrat*, July 31, 1956, B-2, 3.

CHAPTER 9

266. Stover, *Illinois Central Railroad*, 229.
267. Corliss, *Main Line of Mid-America*, 266–69. Like many southern lines, the original gauge was five feet. This was changed in June 1882 to four feet, nine inches instead of the standard four feet, eight and a half inches. Standard-gauge cars could use this line, however. See Stover, *Illinois Central Railroad*, 229.
268. Corliss, *Main Line of Mid-America*, 266–69.
269. Stover, *Illinois Central Railroad*, 229.
270. Corliss, *Main Line of Mid-America*, 268–69; Neuman, *Story of Paducah*, 161. For the right of way, see Thompson, "Paducah Historically," 730–31.
271. Corliss, *Main Line of Mid-America*, 229; also see special edition of the *Paducah Daily News*, January 1, 1888, for a survey of railroads as of that date.
272. Stover, *Illinois Central Railroad*, 296.
273. Ibid., 292, 350–51, 357.
274. Ibid., 364, 454–55.
275. In March 1980, engines from Liberia were under repair in ICG shops at Paducah.
276. *Paducah Sun-Democrat*, December 14, 1950, 1.
277. Mofield, "Atomic Age," 4–6. Mofield was the manager of WPAD Radio in 1950.
278. *Paducah Sun-Democrat*, July 22, 1956, C-12-13.
279. Mofield, "Atomic Age," 19. For the concept of "firm" power involving both hydroelectrics and steam generation, see Twentieth Century Fund (Power Committee), *Electric Power and Government Policy*, 620.
280. The involvement of both TVA and private industry offered an opportunity to test the thesis that private industry is more efficient than would be socialism. TVA was on line before EEI. To name the TVA plant for an Indian tribe that could not maintain a claim to the area is insulting to the memory of the Chickasaw. The only time the Shawnee tried to claim the area was in 1702, under French suggestion. The Shawnee left a trail of bones to mark their retreat.

281. *Paducah Sun-Democrat*, October 17,1951, 1; Mofield, "Atomic Age," 22–23.
282. Mofield, "Atomic Age," 22–23.
283. Ibid., 22.
284. Ibid., 24.
285. Ibid., 29–30.
286. Ibid., 30. About twenty used car lots opened in town.
287. Mofield, "Atomic Age," 31. For a biased view of Paducah, see *Life*, July 14, 1952.
288. Mofield, "Atomic Age," 43, 48–50; interview of Robert Cherry by author, March 6, 1980, audiotape in Paducah Community College Library.
289. Mofield, "Atomic Age," 51–54.
290. Ibid.128–29.
291. Ibid.
292. Ibid., 28–29.
293. Ibid., 34–35.
294. Ibid., 36–37.
295. *Paducah Sun-Democrat*, November 4, 1957, 1.
296. Mofield, "Atomic Age," 38.
297. Ibid., 47–48.
298. Ibid., 58. Chapter IV, "Labor Troubles," is an excellent summary of this troubled period. John Oehlschlaeger was president of the Association of Commerce at the time and heard several prospective company representatives voice concern at the number of illegal strikes in the Paducah area. Interview with the author, March 20,1980.
299. *Business Week*, July 7, 1951,84–86; *Time*, September 15, 1952, 79; *U.S. News and World Report*, October 9, 1953, 84; *Collier's*, June 20, 1953, 70–76.
300. Mofield, "Atomic Age," 60; *Paducah Sun-Democrat*, August 2, 1956, B-3.
301. Mofield, "Atomic Age," 64; *Paducah Sun-Democrat*, August 3, 1956, B-3.
302. Robert Cherry, interview with author, March 6, 1980; Dr. Robert Gordon Matheson, interview with author, March 4, 1980. In one dispute between the steelworkers and the carpenters, the issue was which union was to install windows. Matheson ruled that if the framing was wood, the carpenters would put in the windows. Steel casements were the property of the other union. This type of dispute was common. It was not jurisdictional; rather, it was a union manager problem. Audiotape of the interview with Dr. Matheson is in the library at Paducah Community College.

Chapter 10

303. Hall Allen, "Show Business," *Paducah-Sun Democrat*, July 30, 1956, B-12; Neuman, *Story of Paducah*, "Sports and Amusements," 112–17.
304. There was a local legend that Charles Dickens performed at the St. Clair during his American tour. According to this story, little about the United States impressed the author; however, he took note of a most peculiar house in Paducah. This building was one story, except for the front porch, which had two stories. The improbable architecture was supposed to be mentioned in *Notes on*

American Travels. See Howard, *Paducah, Kentucky*, 6. The building existed. For a time, a historical marker commemorated the visit. Examination of the writings of Dickens disproved the claim, and the marker was removed. See Mitchell, *Historical Points and Places Interesting*, 5. For razing of the St. Clair, see the *Daily News*, May 23, 1895, 2.

305. *Paducah Daily News*, September 26, 1884, 4; November 10, 1884, 4; *Paducah Daily Standard*, October 31, 1886, 4.

306. *Paducah Daily News*, April 21, 1883, 4. Among the males in this performance at St. Clair Hall were C.J. Pearce, W.H. Steele, Andy Weil Jr., H.L. Weil, Rhey Boyd, D.L. Van Gulen, F. Winchester, H.B. Melton, L.G. Orme, Will Perkins, Ike Dallam, Charles Warren and George Rivers. The Concordia Club was a Jewish social organization.

307. *Paducah Daily News*, October 30, 1889, 3.

308. Ibid., October 21, 1900.

309. *Paducah News-Democrat*, September 19, 1901, 8, advertisement.

310. Ibid., September 25, 1901, 8. These shows were followed by Henry Greenwall's *The Gay Mr. Goldstein*, with Thomas Keogh.

311. Allen, "Show Business," B-12, Neuman, *Story of Paducah*, 115–16.

312. *News-Democrat*, December 6, 1905, 3; *Paducah Sun*, April 6, 1906, 2. 4; April 11, 1906, 2.

313. *Paducah Daily News*, December 30, 1874, 4.

314. Ibid., March 10, 1875, 4; July 2, 1877, 4. For the location of the park, see Neuman, *Story of Paducah*, 122.

315. Boswell, *History of Grace Church*, I, 27.

316. Ibid., II, 40.

317. Ibid., 41.

318. Ibid., 41. May was a young girl at the time the diary was kept; she was confirmed on April 29, 1872. See p. 23 for entry.

319. *Daily News*, July 5, 1879, 4. St. Paul's was formed in 1868 and was chartered the following year. Katie Lehrer was the belle of the German community; thus, her wedding was an outstanding social event.

320. Ibid., July 15, 1879, l. The fare had been fifty cents.

321. Ibid., November 10, 1879, 4; April 21, 1888, 5.

322. Ibid., August 1, 1879, 1; August 22, 1879, l. Eisenman's advertisement appeared in the *Daily News*, August 29, 1879, 1.

323. *Daily News*, October 18, 1890, 2.

324. The invoice file of this company was found in a warehouse in 1980. Each regular account was pasted to a section of a page in a large book. As invoices and acceptances arrived, they would be added to the collection. The original is owned by E.B. Michael.

325. Scrapbook is possessed by Mrs. Charlene Hulet of Paducah.

326. *Paducah Daily News*, October 30, 1889, 3; also see November 12, 1889, 3. Tickets in the raffle sold for one dollar.

327. Neuman, *Story of Paducah*, 116–17. According to this account, Rice gave the city its first fire engine in "recognition of kindness bestowed when he was without

funds." For Robinson, see *Paducah Daily News*, June 29, 1888, 2. For Cody, see *Paducah Daily News*, November 20, 21, 1884, 4. Neuman says Cody returned in 1885, 1900 and 1913.

328. Neuman, *Story of Paducah*, August 7, 9, p. l.
329. Ibid.
330. Ibid., August 8, 1905, l.
331. Miller, *Black Patch War*, 49. Miller was the lawyer for the successful plaintiff in the case that broke the power of the Night Riders.
332. Miller, *Black Patch War*, 54–55.
333. *Paducah Daily News-Democrat*, April 23, 24, 1908, 1. Miller says that a company of state guards came to Paducah to protect the city from possible invasion. See Miller, *Black Patch War*, 54–55.
334. Miller, *Black Patch War*, 85; *Paducah Daily News-Democrat*, May 13, 1908, 1; May 14, 1908, l. Also see Nail, *Tobacco Night Riders*.
335. *Paducah Daily News-Democrat*, June 1, 1908, 2. No one seemed to object that Mrs. Flournoy was one of the judges.
336. *Paducah Evening Sun*, November 2, 1901, l; Neuman, *Story of Paducah*, 167.
337. *Paducah News-Democrat*, June 14, 1904, l.
338. Ibid., June 21, 1903, 2.
339. *Paducah Daily News*, February 14, 1879, 4. The temperature was eight degrees above zero, Fahrenheit.
340. *Paducah Daily News*, December 12, 1896, 1.
341. Ibid., June 29, 1883, 4. A common report was that one of the women in the houses would be robbed, as was the case of Ida French. See *Paducah Daily News*, July 26, 1883, 4. Ida claimed that she had been robbed of seven dollars by a railroader who left through the window.
342. *Daily News-Democrat*, May 2, 1903, 6. Tax receipts for the year were the highest in the history of the city; see *Daily News-Democrat*, June 30, 1903, 1. Total tax revenue collected was $12,600.
343. *Daily News-Democrat*, May 5, 1903, 1 for Travelers Protective Association convention. The physicians met on May 10, see also p. 1. The Paducah Gun Club hosted a state meet May 1, see p. 3. The Trimble Street Methodist church had fifty-two conversions at one meeting, see May 4, 1903, 7. For the charges, see June 3, 1903, 1; June 22, 1903, 1. Paducah might have been progressive in 1903, but it still had wooden outhouses in the business district. See *Daily News-Democrat*, May 5, 1903, 3. A cow wandered loose in the downtown area, see May 29, 1903, 7.
344. Quoted in Chidsey, *The Bishop*, 73. Quin arrived in Paducah in March 1911.
345. *Paducah Evening Sun*, July 24, 1916, l. Later, Franklin was made a detective. See July 26, 1916, l.
346. *Paducah Evening Sun*, July 26, 1916, 1. Houses were to close on September 18.
347. *Paducah Evening Sun*, July 27, 1916, l.
348. Ibid., July 31, August 3, 1916, l.
349. Ibid., August 8, 1916, l.
350. Ibid., August 15, 1916, 1, 8.
351. Ibid., September 5, 1916, l.

352. *Paducah News-Democrat*, September 12, 1916, l.
353. *Paducah Evening Sun*, September 19, 20, 21, 1916, l.
354. Ibid., October 19, 1916, l.

CHAPTER 11

355. *Paducah Evening Sun*, October 19, 1916, 476.
356. *Paducah Daily News*, October 23, 1883, 4.
357. Ibid., October 26, 28, 1889, 2.
358. *News-Democrat*, October 14, 1905, 8.
359. *Paducah Evening Sun*, October 17, 1916, l.
360. Ibid., October 31, 1916, l.
361. Glen Murrell, "The Desegregation of Paducah Junior College," *Register* (January 1969): 65.
362. Ibid.
363. Ibid., 66.
364. Ibid., 67.
365. Ibid., 72.
366. Ibid., 76.
367. Ibid., 77. On May 17, 1954, the Supreme Court ruled segregation in schools was unconstitutional in *Brown v. Board of Topeka*, 347 U.S. 483 (1954).
368. Harvey Papers, Paducah, Kentucky.
369. Ibid.
370. Harvey Papers, undated special announcement. A list of the officers of the organization appears in the final paragraph.
371. Harvey Papers, Harvey to Keiler, June 27, 1963.
372. Ibid., Cherry to Lee Livingston and Robert L. Nolan, June 15, 1963; Harvey to Cherry, June 27, 1963.
373. *Paducah Sun-Democrat*, August 9, 1966, l.
374. Ibid., January 27, 1970, 1.
375. Ibid.

BIBLIOGRAPHY

Books and Pamphlets

Alvord, Clarence Walworth. *The Illinois Country: 1673–1881*. Chicago: A.C. McClurg & Co., 1922.

American Annual Cyclopaedia and Register of Important Events. 1861. Reprint, New York: D. Appleton and Co., 1865.

American State Papers. *Class II, Indian Affairs*. Edited by Walter Lowrie and Walter S. Franklin. Washington, D.C.: Gales and Seaton, 1934.

———. *Miscellaneous*. Vol. I. Washington, D.C.: Gales and Seaton, 1934.

Battle, J.H., W.H. Perrin and C.C. Kniffin. *Kentucky: A History of the State*. 2 vols. 1st ed. Louisville, KY: F.A. Battey Publications, 1885. [Volume two is a history of the Purchase region.]

Bernheim, Issac. *The Settlement of Jews in the Lower Ohio Valley*. Pamphlet. Original in the Filson Club, Louisville, KY.

Billington, Ray Allen. *Westward Expansion: A History of the American Frontier*. 2nd ed. New York: MacMillan Co., 1960.

Biographical Directory of the American Congress, 1774–1961. Washington, D.C.: Government Printing Office, 1961.

Borgardus, Carl R., Sr. *The First Steamboat Voyage on the Western Waters*. Au Tin, IN: Muscatatuck Press, 1961. [A reprint of J.H.B. Latrobe's pamphlet published by the Maryland Historical Society in 1871.]

Boswell, Harriett. *History of Grace Church*. 2 vols. MSS, Paducah, ca. 1974. Original at Grace Episcopal Church, Paducah, Kentucky.

Catton, Bruce. *Grant Moves South*. Boston: Little, Brown and Co., 1960.

Chidsey, Alan Lake. *The Bishop: A Portrait of the Right Reverend Clifton S. Quin*. Houston, TX: Gulf Publishing Co., 1966.

Clark, Thomas D. *Frontier America: The Story of the Westward Movement*. New York: Charles Scribner's Sons, 1959.

Collins, Lewis. *History of Kentucky*. 2 vols. Reverend Richard H. Collins (reprint). Frankfort: Kentucky Historical Society, 1966.

Corliss, Carlton J. *Main Line of Mid-America*. New York: Creative Age Press, 1950.

Coulter, Ellis Merton. *The Civil War and Readjustment in Kentucky*. Chapel Hill: University of North Carolina Press, 1926.

Curtis, B.R., ed. *Reports of Decisions of the Supreme Court of the U.S.* Vol. 15. Boston: Little, Brown & Co., 1870.

Deupres, J.G. "The Noxubee Squadron of the First Mississippi Cavalry, C.S.A., 1861–1865." *Publications of the Mississippi Historical Society*. Edited by Dunbar Rowland. Jackson: Mississippi Historical Society, 1918.

English, William Hayden. *Conquest of the Country Northwest of the River Ohio, 1776–1783*. 2 vols. Indianapolis, IN: Brown-Merrill Co., 1897.

Franklin, John Hope. *From Slavery to Freedom: A History of Negro Americans*. 4th ed. New York: Alfred A. Knopf, 1974.

George, Henry, *History of the 3d, 7th, 8th, and 12th Kentucky, C.S.A.* Louisville, KY: C.T. Dearing, n.d. Reprint, Lyndon, KY: Mull-Wathen, 1911,

Grant, Ulysses S. *Personal Memoirs*. 2 vols. New York: Charles L. Webster and Co., 1885.

Grubbs, Millard Dee. *The 4 Keys to Kentucky: Will Unlock the Industrial Financial, Civic, and Political Growth*. Louisville, KY: Stater & Gilroy, 1949.

Howard, Bradford. *Paducah, Kentucky: Its Location, Climate, and Natural Resources*. Paducah, KY: Paducah Evening Sun, 1911. Reprint, 1975.

Hunt, A.L. Papers. Southern Historical Collection, University of North Carolina–Chapel Hill.

James, James Alton. *George Rogers Clark Papers from 1771–1781*. Vol. III, *Illinois Historical Collections*. Edited by Clarence W. Alvord. Part III, *Virginia Series*. Springfield: Illinois State Historical Library, 1912.

Johnson, Robert, and C.C. Buell, eds. *Battles and Leaders of the Civil War*. New York: Century Co., 1887–1888.

Kaufman, Max. *Tales from Specks of Dust: Poems of the Atomic Age*. New York: William-Frederick Press, 1947.

Kerr, Charles, ed. *History of Kentucky*. 5 vols. Chicago: American Historical Society, 1922. [Much of the material is the work of E. Merton Coulter.]

Korn, Bertram Wallace. *American Jewry and the Civil War*. Philadelphia: Jewish Publishing Society of America, 1951.

Malone, James J. *The Chickasaw Nation*. Louisville, KY: John P. Morton and Co., 1922.

Marquette, Jacques. *Journal*. Illinois Historical Collections. Edited by H.W. Beckwith. Springfield, IL: H.W. Rokker Co., 1903.

McClellan, George B. *McClellan's Own Story*. New York: C.L. Webster and Co., 1887.

McElroy, Robert McNutt. *Kentucky in the Nation's History*. New York: Moffat, Yard & Co., 1909.

Memorial Record of Western Kentucky. 2 vols. Chicago: Lewis Publishing Co., 1904.

Military History of Kentucky. Federal WPA project. Frankfort, KY, 1939.

Miller, John G. *The Black Patch War*. Chapel Hill: University of North Carolina Press, 1936.

Mitchell, Robert, Jr. *Historical Points and Places Interesting, Paducah, Kentucky*. Pamphlet. Paducah, KY: Paducah Press, 1948.

Mofield, William Ray. "The Atomic Age Comes to Paducah." Master's thesis. Columbia University, Faculty of Political Science, 1957.

Moore, Frank, ed. *Putnam's Record of the Rebellion*. New York: C.P. Putnam, 1861–1864.

Nall, James O. *The Tobacco Night Riders of Kentucky and Tennessee, 1905–1909*. Louisville, KY: Standard Press, 1939

Neuman, Fred. *The Story of Paducah*. Revised by Catherine Neuman Adams. Paducah, KY: Image Graphics, 1979. [The original was in 1927.]

Paducah City Directory for 1890–1891. Evansville, IN: Bennett and Co., 1891.

Paxson, Frederick L. *History of the American Frontier: 1763–1893*. Boston: Houghton Mifflin Co., 1924.

Pell, Edna S. *The Descendents of William Pell, Sr. of Kent County, Maryland*. Paducah, KY: self-published, 1968.

Report of the Adjutant General of the State of Kentucky: Confederate Kentucky Volunteers War 1861–1865. Frankfort, KY: State Journal Co., 1915.

Sames, James Walter. *Four Steps West: A History of the Boundary Between Virginia and North Carolina and Kentucky and Tennessee*. Versailles, KY: self-published, 1971.

Sandburg, Carl. *Abraham Lincoln: The Prairie Years and the War Years*. Pleasantville, NY: Readers' Digest Illustrated Edition by arrangement with Harcourt Brace Javanovich, Inc., 1970.

Shannon, Jasper B., and Ruth McQuown. *Presidential Politics in Kentucky, 1824–1948*. Lexington: University of Kentucky Press, 1950.

South Central Bell Telephone Directory. "The Purchase." Paducah, KY, 1979.

Stickles, Arndt. *Simon Bolivar Buckner*. Chapel Hill: University of North Carolina Press, 1940.

Stover, John F. *History of the Illinois Central Railroad*. New York: McMillian Publishing Co., 1975.

Summers, Lewis Preston. *History of Southwestern Virginia, 1746–1786; Washington County, 1777–1780*. Richmond, VA: J.C. Hill Printing Co., 1903.

Thompson, Edward Porter. *History of the Orphan Brigade*. Louisville, KY: Lewis N. Thompson, 1898.

Thompson, H.E. "Paducah Historically." In *Constitution and Revision of the Ordinances and Municipal Laws of the City of Paducah, Kentucky, Under the Charter of March 19, 1894, and Amendments Thereto*. Paducah, KY: Young Printing Co., 1910.

Twentieth Century Fund (Power Committee). *Electric Power and Government Policy*. New York: Twentieth Century Fund, 1948.

U.S. House of Representatives. *Freedman's Affairs in Kentucky and Tennessee*. 40th Congress, 2nd Session. Exec. Doc. 329.

War of the Rebellion: Official Records of the Union and Confederate Armies. Washington, D.C.: Government Printing Office, 1871.

Williams' Paducah Directory, City Guide and Business Mirror. Paducah, KY: Byers and Clements, 1859.

Williams, Stephen K., ed. *Reports of Cases Argued and Decided in the Supreme Court of the U.S.* Book XI, cont How Vols. 1, 2, 3, 4. Newark, NY: Lawyer's Co-Op Publishing Co., 1883.

Winsor, Justin. *The Westward Movement.* Cambridge. MA: Riverside Press, 1897.

MAGAZINES AND ARTICLES

Business Week, July 1951.

Colliers, June 20, 1953.

Hamilton, Holeman. "Kentucky's Linn Boyd and the Dramatic Days of 1850." *Register* 55 (n.d.).

Murrell, Glen. "The Desegregation of Paducah Junior College." *Register* 67 (January 1969).

National Geographic, June 1973.

Robertson, John E.L. "Fort Jefferson." *Register* 71 (April 1973).

———. "Paducah: Origins to Second Class." *Register* 66 (April 1968).

Time, September 15, 1952.

U.S. News and World Report, October 9, 1953.

GOVERNMENT DOCUMENTS

Acts of Kentucky, 1821; 1822–23; 1822–23; 1823–24; 1825; 1856, Public; 1859; 1861; 1862; 1871; 1873.

Kentucky Documents, 1861.

Kentucky House Journal, 1861

Kentucky Reports, Vol. 171, 1916.

Kentucky Senate and House Journal, 1865

Kentucky Senate Journal, 1865

Livingston County, Deed Book E.

McCracken County, Deed Book A, 56.

McCracken Circuit Court, *Burns v. Lackey*, Box 1271.

Paducah Order Books. Minutes of the Council.

Rev. Stat. of Kentucky, 1904.

Seventh Census, 1850. Kentucky, Vol. 14, by N.M. McCurty. July 25, 1850. Microfilm, M-2, vol. 15. Mason to Monroe.

COLLECTIONS

Burnham Papers, Paducah [This collection consists of over three boxes measuring three feet long by one foot wide and one foot deep. Most of the information came from Paducah order books, deed books, newspapers, etc. Newspaper items do not have page numbers.]

Draper MSS, Wisconsin Historical Collection

Goodman Papers, Margaret I. King Library, University of Kentucky, Lexington [Goodman was from Paducah and owner of the *News-Democrat*. He also headed the WPA for Kentucky.]

Harvey Papers, Paducah [Reverend Harvey was the first black to serve on the Paducah City Commission.]

Jackson Papers, Library of Congress, Washington, D.C. Microfilm, Reel 62 A, Jackson, Treaty, 1818. Series III, Letters and Orders, 1813–1822. 15 vols. "A-O."

NEWSPAPERS

Cairo [Illinois] Delta. Microfilm, Cairo Public Library.

Louisville Daily Courier, 1861. Microfilm.

Louisville Journal, 1861. Microfilm.

Paducah Newspapers

Christian Banner. [Elder J.R. Howard. Christian Church.]

Commercial, 1859. [Whig. William Roleston.]

Daily Republican, 1888.

Democrat, 1901. [Urey Woodson. Absorbed the *Daily News*.]

Dollar Times, ca. 1857. [W.L. Geary.]

Evening Eye, 1887.

Evening Sun, 1896. [Frank M. Fisher. Republican. Merged on May 1, 1929 with the *Democrat* to form the *Sun-Democrat*.]

Express, 1834–35. [R.R. Willis. Whig.]

Federal Union, 1861–65. [Army issue using plant of Noble.]

Kentuckian, 1872. [Originally the *Herald*.]

Labor Chronicle, 1890.

Leader. [James R. Lemon.]

Ledger. [Good Government League.]

Moon, 1889.

News, 1871. [Thaddeus C. Ballard and James P. Thompson. Lasted until 1901, when it merged with the *Democrat*.]

Paducah American. [Know-Nothing. Perry & McGoodwin.]

Paducah Daily Enterprise. [John B. Gaines.]

Paducah Daily News. [Ballard and Thompson.]

Paducah Democrat, 1851. [C.C. Riley. R.B.J. Twyman took over later and enlarged.]

Paducah Herald, 1857. [Democrat. John G. Noble. Closed by Federal forces during the Civil War. Issued also as a tri-weekly to 1861. The paper was revived in 1865 and lasted until 1872.]

Paducah Journal, 1849. [Whig. H.M. McCarty and R.W. Perry. Sold in 1855 to J. Stoddard Byers and Reverend W.W. Dodd, who leased the paper to D.W. McCarty and F.W. Thomas. Failed in 1856.]

Paducah Republican, 1887.

Paducah Sentinel, ca. 1854. [Whig. John D. McGoodwin.]

Paducah Union, 1887.

Pennant, 1853. [Whig. Samuel Pike. Sold in 1854 to George H. Morrow, who kept for a short time and transferred to Perry & McGoodin, which changed its name.]

Register. [James E. Wilhelm.]

Standard, 1884. [Charles O.C., Edward O., Oliver P. and Clinton R. Leigh.]

Sunday Truth, 1891.

Sunday Visitor.

Truth, 1891.

Voice of the People. [Labor Daily. George Morris. This was the official city newspaper in 1917–18.]

Weekly Truth, 1887.

West Kentuckian. [Weekly. J.A. Blake.]

West Kentuckian, 1844. [John McKay Lambdin. Whig. Sold to William Grief. Sold in 1849 and name changed.]

INDEX

C

E

F

M

N

O

P

S

Y

Z

ABOUT THE AUTHOR

John E.L. Robertson is professor emeritus of the University of Kentucky Community College system and was recognized as historian of the year by the Kentucky Historical Society in 2008.